Non-League
Football
Supporters'
Guide
& Yearbook
2021

EDITOR
Steve Askew

Twenty-ninth Edition

For details of our range of over 2,400 books and almost 300 DVDs, visit our web site or contact us using the information shown below.

British Library Cataloguing in Publication Data
A catalogue record for this book is available from the British Library

ISBN: 978-1-86223-429-1

Copyright © 2020, SOCCER BOOKS LIMITED (01472 696226)
72 St. Peter's Avenue, Cleethorpes, N.E. Lincolnshire, DN35 8HU, England

Web site www.soccer-books.co.uk • e-mail info@soccer-books.co.uk

The Publishers, and the Football Clubs itemised are unable to accept liability for any loss, damage or injury caused by error or inaccuracy in the information published in this guide.

Manufactured in the UK by Severn.

FOREWORD

Following the unprecedented effects of the Covid-19 pandemic, the 2019/2020 season in the National League was suspended on 16th March 2020 before ending on 20th April 2020 when it was clear that no further play would be possible. On 17th June 2020, the member clubs decided that final league positions would be calculated on a points per game basis so the teams finishing top of each division therefore won promotion. Promotion play-offs were held in July and August to decide the additional promotion places. There was no relegation into or promotion from the Leagues in Step 3 of the pyramid this season.

At the time of going to press, it was unclear when fans would again be allowed to attend matches. Quite understandably, therefore, many clubs had not decided their admission charges for the coming season. If in doubt, we would suggest contacting clubs before attending games (once this is possible) to discover pricing and other relevant requirements.

Following the winding-up of Macclesfield Town FC by the High Court, we have removed information for the club from this guide. We sincerely hope that, given the ongoing problems caused by the Covid-19 pandemic, no other National League clubs will find themselves in the same position.

Our thanks go to the numerous club officials who have aided us in the compilation of information contained in this guide as well as Michael Robinson (page layouts) and Bob Budd (cover artwork).

Any readers who have up-to-date ground photographs which they would like us to consider for use in a future edition of this guide are requested to contact us at our address which is shown on the facing page.

The fixtures listed later in this book were released just a short time before we went to print and, as such, some of the dates shown may be subject to change. We therefore suggest that readers treat these fixtures as a rough guide and check dates carefully before attending matches.

We would like to wish our readers a safe and happy spectating season.

Steve Askew
EDITOR

CONTENTS

THE VANARAMA NATIONAL LEAGUE

Address   4th Floor, 20 Waterloo Street, Birmingham   B2 5TB

Phone (0121) 643-3143

Web site   www.footballconference.co.uk

Clubs for the 2020/2021 Season

ALDERSHOT TOWN FC

Founded: 2013 (as a new company)
Former Names: Aldershot Town FC
Nickname: 'Shots'
Ground: Ebb Stadium, High Street, Aldershot, GU11 1TW
Record Attendance: 7,500 (18th November 2000)
Pitch Size: 117 × 76 yards

Colours: Red shirts with Blue Sleeves, Blue shorts
Telephone N°: (01252) 320211
Club Secretary: (01252) 320211– Bob Green
Ground Capacity: 7,100
Seating Capacity: 2,136
Web site: www.theshots.co.uk
E-mail: admin@theshots.co.uk

GENERAL INFORMATION

Car Parking: Parsons Barracks Car Park is adjacent
Coach Parking: Contact the club for information
Nearest Railway Station: Aldershot (5 mins. walk)
Nearest Bus Station: Aldershot (5 minutes walk)
Club Shop: At the ground
Opening Times: Weekdays 10.00am to 4.00pm, Saturday matchdays 10.00am to 2.45pm and 9.30am to 7.30pm on Tuesday matchdays. Times may be subject to change.
Telephone N°: (01252) 320211

GROUND INFORMATION

Away Supporters' Entrances & Sections:
For unsegregated games, please use Turnstile 4 for accommodation in the Community Stand. For segregated games, accommodation will be in the South East Corner of the Stadium and The Bill Warren seats, in the South Stand.

ADMISSION INFO (2020/2021 PRICES)

Adult Standing/Seating: £20.00
Ages 11 to 18 Standing: £5.00
Ages 11 to 18 Seating: £7.00
Note: Under-11s are admitted free with paying adults – a maximum of 2 children per adult.
Concessionary Standing: £14.00
Concessionary Seating: £16.00
Note: Military personnel are charged Concessionary prices
Programme Price: Please contact the club for details.

DISABLED INFORMATION

Wheelchairs: Accommodated in both the North Stand and the away section (Away fans use gate 45).
Helpers: Admitted
Prices: Concessionary prices for the disabled. Helpers free.
Disabled Toilets: Available
Contact: (01252) 320211 (Bookings are required)

Travelling Supporters' Information:
Routes: From the M3: Exit at Junction 4 and follow signs for Aldershot (A331). Leave the A331 at the A323 exit (Ash Road) and continue along into the High Street. The ground is just past the Railway Bridge on the right; From the A31: Continue along the A31 to the junction with the A331, then as above; From the A325 (Farnborough Road): Follow signs to the A323 then turn left into Wellington Avenue. The ground is just off the 2nd roundabout on the left – the floodlights are clearly visible.

ALTRINCHAM FC

Founded: 1891
Former Names: Broadheath FC
Nickname: 'The Robins'
Ground: The J.Davidson Stadium, Moss Lane,
Altrincham   WA15 8AP
Record Attendance: 10,275 (February 1925)
Pitch Size: 110 × 72 yards
Web site: www.altrinchamfc.com

Colours: Red and White striped shirts, Black shorts
Telephone N°: (0161) 928-1045
Ground Capacity: 6,085
Seating Capacity: 1,323
E-mail: office@altrinchamfootballclub.co.uk

GENERAL INFORMATION

Car Parking: The club has an agreement for supporters to use the Aecom car park (179 Moss Lane, WA14 8FH) on matchdays. This is just a short walk from the stadium.
Coach Parking: By Police Direction
Nearest Railway Station: Altrincham (15 minutes walk)
Nearest Bus Station: Altrincham
Club Shop: Inside the ground
Opening Times: Weekdays 9.00am to 5.00pm
Telephone N°: (0161) 928-1045

GROUND INFORMATION

Away Supporters' Entrances & Sections:
Hale End turnstiles and accommodation

ADMISSION INFO (2019/2020 PRICES)

Adult Standing/Seating: £14.00
Senior Citizen/Student Standing/Seating: £11.00
Under-16s Standing/Seating: £5.00
Under-12s Standing/Seating: £1.00

DISABLED INFORMATION

Wheelchairs: 3 spaces are available each for home and away fans adjacent to the Away dugout
Helpers: Admitted
Prices: Normal prices apply for disabled supporters. Helpers are admitted free of charge
Disabled Toilets: Yes
Contact: (0161) 928-1045   (Bookings are necessary)

Travelling Supporters' Information:
Routes: Exit the M56 at either Junction 6 or 7 and follow the signs for Altrincham FC.

BARNET FC

Founded: 1888
Former Names: Barnet Alston FC
Nickname: 'The Bees'
Ground: The Hive, Camrose Avenue, Edgware, HA8 6AG
Record Attendance: 6,215 (29th January 2019)
Pitch Size: 112 × 73 yards

Colours: Shirts and shorts are Black and Amber
Telephone N°: (020) 8381-3800
Ticket Office: (020) 8381-3800
Ground Capacity: 6,500
Seating Capacity: 5,419
Web site: www.barnetfc.com
E-mail: tellus@barnetfc.com

GENERAL INFORMATION

Car Parking: 350 spaces available at the ground
Coach Parking: Available at the ground
Nearest Railway Station: Harrow & Wealdstone (2½ miles)
Nearest Tube Station: Canons Park (5 minutes walk)
Club Shop: At the ground
Opening Times: Daily from 8.00am to 11.00pm – the shop is open throughout The Hive opening hours.
Telephone N°: (020) 8381-3800

GROUND INFORMATION

Away Supporters' Entrances & Sections:
North Terrace and North West corner

ADMISSION INFO (2020/2021 PRICES)

Adult Standing: £15.00
Adult Seating: £22.00
Concessionary Standing: £10.00
Concessionary Seating: £14.00
Under-17s Standing: £1.00
Under-17s Seating: £5.00
Programme Price: £3.00

FANS WITH DISABILITIES INFORMATION

Wheelchairs: 42 covered spaces in total for Home and Away fans in the East and West Stands
Helpers: One helper admitted per wheelchair
Prices: Normal prices for fans with disabilities. Helpers free
Disabled Toilets: Available
Contact: (020) 8381-3800 (Bookings are advisable)

Travelling Supporters' Information:
Routes: Exit the M1 at Junction 4 and take the Edgware Way/Watford Bypass (A41). Take the 3rd exit at the roundabout onto the A410 then the first exit at the next roundabout along the A5 (Stonegrove), continuing for approximately 1½ miles. Turn right into Camrose Avenue and The Hive is approximately two-thirds of a mile along this road.

BOREHAM WOOD FC

Founded: 1948
Former Names: Boreham Rovers FC and Royal Retournez FC
Nickname: 'The Wood'
Ground: Meadow Park, Broughinge Road, Borehamwood, Hertfordshire WD6 5AL
Record Attendance: 4,030 (2001 vs Arsenal)
Pitch Size: 112 × 72 yards

Colours: White shirts and shorts
Telephone N°: (0208) 953-5097
Fax Number: (0208) 207-7982
Ground Capacity: 4,500
Seating Capacity: 1,700
Web site: www.borehamwoodfootballclub.co.uk

GENERAL INFORMATION

Car Parking: Brook Road car park is nearby
Coach Parking: Please contact the club for details
Nearest Railway Station: Elstree & Borehamwood (1 mile)
Nearest Bus Station: Barnet
Club Shop: At the ground
Opening Times: 9.00am to 10.00pm Monday to Thursday; 9.00am to 6.00pm at weekends
Telephone N°: (0208) 953-5097

GROUND INFORMATION

Away Supporters' Entrances & Sections:
Use the Away Gate in the West Stand for access to South Stand accommodation.

ADMISSION INFO (2020/2021 PRICES)

Adult Standing/Seating: £20.00
Under-16s Standing/Seating: £10.00
Under-12s Standing/Seating: £5.00
Senior Citizen Standing/Seating: £15.00
Note:: Tickets are £2.00 cheaper when purchased in advance online (£3.00 cheaper for Under-12s).

DISABLED INFORMATION

Wheelchairs: Accommodated in the West Stand
Helpers: Admitted
Prices: Normal prices are charged for the disabled. Helpers are admitted free of charge.
Disabled Toilets: Available
Contact: (0208) 953-5097 (Bookings are not necessary)

Travelling Supporters' Information:
Routes: Exit the M25 at Junction 23 and take the A1 South. After 2 miles, take the Borehamwood exit onto the dual carriageway and go over the flyover following signs for Borehamwood for 1 mile. Turn right at the Studio roundabout into Brook Road, then next right into Broughinge Road for the ground.

BROMLEY FC

Founded: 1892
Former Names: None
Nickname: 'Lillywhites' 'The Ravens'
Ground: The Stadium, Hayes Lane, Bromley, Kent, BR2 9EF
Record Attendance: 10,798 (24th September 1949)
Pitch Size: 112 × 72 yards

Colours: White shirts with Black shorts
Telephone N°: (020) 8460-5291
Ground Capacity: 5,000
Seating Capacity: 1,300
Web site: www.bromleyfc.tv
E-mail: info@bromleyfc.co.uk

GENERAL INFORMATION

Car Parking: 300 spaces available at the ground
Coach Parking: At the ground
Nearest Railway Station: Bromley South (1 mile)
Nearest Bus Station: High Street, Bromley
Club Shop: At the ground
Opening Times: Matchdays only
Telephone N°: (020) 8460-5291

GROUND INFORMATION

Away Supporters' Entrances & Sections:
No usual segregation

ADMISSION INFO (2020/2021 PRICES)

Adult Standing/Seating: £15.00 (£18.00)
Concessionary Standing/Seating: £10.00 (£12.00)
Under-16s/Student Standing/Seating: £5.00 (£10.00)
Note: Prices shown are for tickets purchased in advance. Tickets purchased just before the game are more expensive (prices shown above in brackets). Discounted prices are available on the matchday for online bookings before 1.30pm or 6.30pm for day and night matches respectively. Under-16s are admitted free of charge with a paying adult for advance purchases up to 1 hour before kick-off.
A special £10.00 discounted price is available for Season Ticket holders of Premiership and Football League clubs.

DISABLED INFORMATION

Wheelchairs: Accommodated
Prices: Concessionary prices are charged for disabled fans. Helpers are admitted free of charge
Disabled Toilets: Available
Contact: (0181) 460-5291 (Bookings are necessary) – David Cook (Disabled Liaison Officer) – 07786 068569

Travelling Supporters' Information:
Routes: Exit the M25 at Junction 4 and follow the A21 for Bromley and London for approximately 4 miles before forking left onto the A232 signposted for Croydon/Sutton. At the second set of traffic lights turn right into Baston Road (B265) and follow for approximately 2 miles as it becomes Hayes Street and then Hayes Lane. The ground is on the right just after a mini-roundabout.

CHESTERFIELD FC

Founded: 1866
Former Names: Chesterfield Municipal FC, Chesterfield Town FC
Nickname: 'Spireites' 'Blues'
Ground: Technique Stadium , 1866 Sheffield Road, Whittington Moor, Chesterfield   S41 8NZ
Ground Capacity: 10,500 (All seats)

Record Attendance: 30,968 (Saltergate – 7/4/1939)
Pitch Size: 112 × 71 yards
Colours: Blue shirts with White shorts
Telephone N°: (01246) 269300
Ticket Office: (01246) 269300 (Option 1)
Web Site: www.chesterfield-fc.co.uk

GENERAL INFORMATION

Car Parking: Various Car Parks available nearby
Coach Parking: At the ground
Nearest Railway Station: Chesterfield (1¼ miles)
Nearest Bus Station: Chesterfield
Club Shop: At the ground
Opening Times: Please contact the club for details
Telephone N°: (01246) 209765

GROUND INFORMATION

Away Supporters' Entrances & Sections:
H. Lilleker North Stand Turnstiles

ADMISSION INFO (2020/2021 PRICES)

Adult Seating: £18.00 – £22.00
Ages 17 to 21 Seating: £11.00 – £15.00
Juvenile (Under-17s) Seating: £7.00
Concessionary Seating: £14.00 – £18.00
Under-7s Seating: £5.00 in the Family Stand
Programme Price: £3.00

FANS WITH DISABILITIES INFORMATION

Wheelchairs: Up to 100 spaces available around the ground
Note: Lifts are available in the East and West stands
Helpers: One helper admitted per fan with disabilities
Prices: Normal prices for disabled fans. Free for helpers.
Disabled Toilets: Available in all stands
Contact: (01246) 269300 Ext. 6002 (Bookings are advised)
John Croot (Disabled Liaiison Officer) –
johncroot@chesterfield-fc.co.uk

Travelling Supporters' Information:
Routes: From the South: Exit the M1 at Junction 29 and follow the A617 for Chesterfield. At the roundabout, take the 4th exit and head north on the A61 Sheffield Road and the stadium is located in the Whittington Moor district next to the junction with the A619; From the East: Take the A619 to Chesterfield and the ground is situated next to the Tesco supermarket at the junction with the A61; From the North: Exit the M1 at Junction 30 and take the A619 to Chesterfield. Then as above.

DAGENHAM & REDBRIDGE FC

Founded: 1992 **(Entered League**: 2007)
Former Names: Formed by the merger of
Dagenham FC and Redbridge Forest FC
Nickname: 'The Daggers'
Ground: Chigwell Construction Stadium,
Victoria Road, Dagenham RM10 7XL
Record Attendance: 5,949 (vs Ipswich Town in 2002)
Pitch Size: 110 × 70 yards

Colours: Red shirts with Blue shorts
Telephone Nº: (020) 8592-1549
Ticket Office: (020) 8592-1549 (Ext. 2)
Fax Number: (020) 8593-7227
Ground Capacity: 6,078
Seating Capacity: 2,233
Web site: www.daggers.co.uk
E-mail: info@daggers.co.uk

GENERAL INFORMATION

Car Parking: Street parking only
Coach Parking: Street parking only
Nearest Railway Station: Dagenham East (5 mins. walk)
Nearest Bus Station: Romford
Club Shop: At the ground
Opening Times: Monday & Tuesday 12.00pm – 4.00pm;
Thursday 12.00pm – 8.00pm; Friday 12.00pm – 6.00pm;
Saturday matchdays 1.00pm – 3.00pm.
Closed on Wednesdays, Sundays and non-match Saturdays
Telephone Nº: (020) 8592-7194

GROUND INFORMATION

Away Supporters' Entrances & Sections:
Pondfield Road entrances for West Stand accommodation

ADMISSION INFO (2020/2021 PRICES)

Adult Standing: £15.00
Adult Seating: £15.00 – £21.00
Concessionary Standing: £10.00
Concessionary Seating: £10.00 – £15.00
Under-16s Standing: £8.00 (Under-10s free of charge)
Under-16s Seating: £8.00 – £12.00
Under-10s Seating: £2.00 (Free in the Family Stand)

DISABLED INFORMATION

Wheelchairs: Accommodated in front of the new Stand
and the Family Stand
Helpers: Admitted
Prices: £15.00 for the disabled. Free of charge for Helpers
Disabled Toilets: Available at the East and West ends of the
ground and also in the Clubhouse
Contact: (020) 8592-7194 Ext. 4 (Bookings are necessary)
Tony Payne (Club Secretary) – secretary@daggers.co.uk

Travelling Supporters' Information:
Routes: From the North & West: Take the M11 to its end and join the A406 South. At the large roundabout take the slip road
on the left signposted A13 to Dagenham. As you approach Dagenham, stay in the left lane and follow signs for A1306 signposted
Dagenham East. Turn left onto the A1112 at the 5th set of traffic lights by the McDonalds. Proceed along Ballards Road to The
Bull roundabout and bear left. Victoria Road is 450 yards on the left after passing Dagenham East tube station; From the South
& East: Follow signs for the A13 to Dagenham. Take the next slip road off signposted Elm Park & Dagenham East then turn right
at the roundabout. Go straight on at the next roundabout and turn left onto A1306. After ½ mile you will see a McDonalds on
the right. Get into the right hand filter lane and turn right onto A1112. Then as from the North & West.   **SatNav**: RM10 7XL

DOVER ATHLETIC FC

Founded: 1983
Former Names: None
Nickname: 'The Whites'
Ground: Crabble Athletic Ground, Lewisham Road, River, Dover CT17 0JB
Record Attendance: 7,000 (vs Folkestone in 1951)
Pitch Size: 111 × 73 yards

Colours: White shirts with Black shorts
Telephone N°: (01304) 822373
Fax Number: (01304) 821383
Ground Capacity: 5,745
Seating Capacity: 1,500
Web site: www.doverathletic.com
E-mail: enquiries@doverathletic.com

GENERAL INFORMATION
Car Parking: Street parking
Coach Parking: Street parking
Nearest Railway Station: Kearsney (1 mile)
Nearest Bus Station: Pencester Road, Dover (1½ miles)
Club Shop: At the ground
Opening Times: Saturdays 9.00am to 12.00pm
Telephone N°: (01304) 822373

GROUND INFORMATION
Away Supporters' Entrances & Sections:
Segregation only used when required

ADMISSION INFO (2020/2021 PRICES)
Adult Standing/Seating: £18.00
Concessionary Standing/Seating: £15.00

DISABLED INFORMATION
Wheelchairs: Approximately 6 spaces are available in the Family Stand
Helpers: Admitted
Prices: Normal prices are applied for the disabled, helpers are admitted free of charge.
Disabled Toilets: Three available
Contact: (01304) 822373 (Bookings are not necessary)

Travelling Supporters' Information:
Routes: Take the A2 to the Whitfield roundabout and take the 4th exit. Travel down the hill to the mini-roundabout then turn left and follow the road for 1 mile to the traffic lights on the hill. Turn sharp right and pass under the railway bridge – the ground is on the left after 300 yards.

EASTLEIGH FC

Founded: 1946	**Colours**: Blue shirts, shorts and socks
Former Names: Swaythling Athletic FC and Swaythling FC	**Telephone N°**: (023) 8061-3361
Nickname: 'The Spitfires'	**Fax Number**: (023) 8061-2379
Ground: The Silverlake Stadium, Stoneham Lane, Eastleigh SO50 9HT	**Ground Capacity**: 5,192
	Seating Capacity: 3,210
	Web site: www.eastleighfc.com
Record Attendance: 5,025 (2016 vs Bolton Wands.)	**e-mail**: admin@eastleighfc.com
Pitch Size: 112 × 74 yards	

GENERAL INFORMATION

Car Parking: Spaces for 450 cars (hard standing – £5.00)
Coach Parking: At the ground
Nearest Railway Station: Southampton Parkway (¾ mile)
Nearest Bus Station: Eastleigh (2 miles)
Club Shop: At the ground
Opening Times: Monday to Friday 10.00am to 4.00pm plus Saturday and Weekdays Matchdays 9.00am until kick-off, then for 30 minutes after the game.
Telephone N°: (023) 8061-3361

GROUND INFORMATION

Away Supporters' Entrances & Sections:
Mackoy Community Stand, Blocks 1, 2 & 3 – entrance via Turnstiles 10 and 11

ADMISSION INFO (2020/2021 PRICES)

Adult Standing: £12.00   **Adult Seating**: £15.00
Concessionary Standing: £8.00
Concessionary Seating: £10.00
Under-18s Standing: £4.00   **Under-18s Seating**: £5.00
Under-11s Standing/Seating: Free of charge
Note: Discounted prices are available for advance purchases

DISABLED INFORMATION

Wheelchairs: 24 spaces for home fans in the Mackoy (South) Stand plus 2 in the West Stand. A further 7 spaces are available in the Mackoy Stand for away fans.
Helpers: Admitted
Prices: Normal prices for the disabled. Helpers free of charge
Disabled Toilets: Available
Contact: (023) 8061-3361   (Bookings are not necessary) – Sarah Woolley – dlo@eastleighfc.com

Travelling Supporters' Information:
Routes: Exit the M27 at Junction 5 (signposted for Southampton Airport) and take the A335 (Stoneham Way) towards Southampton. After ½ mile, turn right at the traffic lights into Bassett Green Road. Turn right at the next set of traffic lights into Stoneham Lane and the ground is on the right after ¾ mile.

FC HALIFAX TOWN

Founded: 1911 (Re-formed 2008)	**Record Attendance**: 8,042 (vs Bradford City, 2014)
Former Names: Halifax Town FC	**Pitch Size**: 112 × 73 yards
Nickname: 'The Shaymen'	**Colours**: Blue shirts and shorts
Ground: The Shay Stadium, Shay Syke, Halifax, HX1 2YT	**Telephone Nº**: (01422) 341222
Ground Capacity: 10,568	**Fax Number**: (01422) 349487
Seating Capacity: 5,285	**Web Site**: www.fchalifaxtown.co.uk
	E-mail: tonyallan@fchalifaxtown.co.uk

GENERAL INFORMATION

Car Parking: Adjacent to the East Stand and also Shaw Hill Car Park (Nearby)
Coach Parking: By arrangement with the Club Secretary
Nearest Railway Station: Halifax (10 minutes walk)
Nearest Bus Station: Halifax (15 minutes walk)
Club Shop: At the ground in the East Stand
Opening Times: Please phone for details
Telephone Nº: (01422) 341222

GROUND INFORMATION

Away Supporters' Entrances & Sections:
Skircoat Stand (Seating only)

ADMISSION INFO (2020/2021 PRICES)

Adult Standing/Seating: £20.00
Senior Citizen Standing/Seating: £17.00
Under-18s Standing/Seating: £9.00
Under-12s Standing/Seating: £5.00
Under-7s Standing/Seating: £3.00

DISABLED INFORMATION

Wheelchairs: 33 spaces available in total in disabled sections in the East Stand on the 2nd & 3rd tier levels
Helpers: One admitted free with each paying disabled fan
Prices: Free of charge for the disabled and helpers
Disabled Toilets: Available in the East Stand, both levels
Contact: (01422) 886802 (Bookings are not necessary)
Ken Cheslett – ken_chesd@hotmail.co.uk

Travelling Supporters' Information:
Routes: From the North: Take the A629 to Halifax Town Centre. Take the 2nd exit at the roundabout into Broad Street and follow signs for Huddersfield (A629) into Skircoat Road; From the South, East and West: Exit the M62 at Junction 24 and follow Halifax (A629) signs for the Town Centre into Skircoat Road then Shaw Hill for ground. **SatNav**: Use HX1 2YS for the ground.

HARTLEPOOL UNITED FC |

Founded: 1908
Former Names: Hartlepools United FC (1908-68); Hartlepool FC (1968-77)
Nickname: 'The Pool' 'Pools'
Ground: Victoria Park, Clarence Road, Hartlepool TS24 8BZ
Ground Capacity: 7,865 **Seating Capacity**: 4,359
Record Attendance: 17,426 (15th January 1957)

Pitch Size: 110 × 74 yards
Colours: Blue and White shirts with Blue shorts
Telephone Nº: (01429) 272584
Ticket Office: (01429) 272584 Option 2
Ticket Office e-mail: tickets@hartlepoolunited.co.uk
Fax Number: (01429) 863007
Web Site: www.hartlepoolunited.co.uk
E-mail: enquiries@hartlepoolunited.co.uk

GENERAL INFORMATION
Car Parking: Limited space at the ground (£5.00 charge) and also street parking
Coach Parking: Church Street
Nearest Railway Station: Hartlepool Church Street (5 minutes walk)
Club Shop: At the ground
Opening Times: Monday to Friday 10.00am to 4.00pm and Saturday Matchdays 10.00am to 3.00pm.
Telephone Nº: (01429) 272584

GROUND INFORMATION
Away Supporters' Entrances & Sections:
Clarence Road turnstiles 1 & 2 for Smith & Graham Stand

ADMISSION INFO (2020/2021 PRICES)
Adult Standing: £18.00
Adult Seating: £20.00
Senior Citizen/Under-19s/Student Standing: £9.00
Senior Citizen/Under-19s/Student Seating: £10.00
Under-16s: Admitted for £5.00 with a paying adult
Programme Price: £3.00

DISABLED INFORMATION
Wheelchairs: 14 spaces for Home fans in disabled section, Camerons CK Stand, 10 spaces for Away fans in the Smith & Graham Stand.
Helpers: One helper admitted per wheelchair
Prices: Normal prices for disabled fans. Helpers free of charge
Disabled Toilets: Available around the ground
Contact: (01429) 272584 Option 9 (Bookings advisable): Neil Appleyard (0774 7735247) neilappleyard@hotmail.com

Travelling Supporters' Information: **Routes**: From the North: Take the A1/A19 to the A179 and follow Town Centre/ Marina signs. Turn right at the roundabout by the 'Historic Quayside' and cross over the Railway bridge. The ground is on the left; From the South & West: Take the A689 following Town Centre/Marina signs. Turn left at the roundabout by the 'Historic Quayside' and cross over the Railway bridge. The ground is on the left.

KING'S LYNN TOWN FC

Founded: 1879
Former Names: Lynn Town FC, Lynn FC
Nickname: 'The Linnets'
Ground: The Walks Stadium, Tennyson Road, King's Lynn   PE30 5PB
Record Attendance: 12,937 (vs Exeter City 1950/51)
Pitch Size: 115 × 78 yards

Colours: Blue shirts with Yellow trim, Blue shorts
Telephone N°: (01553) 760060
Fax Number: (01553) 762159
Ground Capacity: 8,200
Seating Capacity: 1,200
Web site: www.kltown.co.uk
E-mail: office@kltown.co.uk

GENERAL INFORMATION
Car Parking: 100 spaces available at the ground
Coach Parking: At the ground
Nearest Railway Station: King's Lynn (¼ mile)
Nearest Bus Station: King's Lynn (¼ mile)
Club Shop: At the ground
Opening Times: Matchdays only
Telephone N°: (01553) 760060

GROUND INFORMATION
Away Supporters' Entrances & Sections:
No usual segregation but away fans should use the North East Corner when segregation is in force.

ADMISSION INFO (2020/2021 PRICES)
Adult Standing: £20.00
Adult Seating: £22.00 – £25.00
Concessions Standing: £18.00
Concessions Seating: £20.00 – £25.00
Under-16s Standing: £5.00
Under-16s Seating: £10.00

DISABLED INFORMATION
Wheelchairs: Accommodated
Helpers: Please phone the club for information
Prices: Please phone the club for information
Disabled Toilets: Available
Contact: (01553) 760060   (Bookings are not necessary)

Travelling Supporters' Information:
Routes: From all directions: The A47/A17/A10 all meet at Hardwick Roundabout. At this roundabout follow signs for the town centre passing through two sets of traffic lights. After the second set of lights get in the right hand lane and take the 4th exit at the roundabout keeping the Car Sales outlet on the left. Continue for ½ mile into Tennyson Road and the ground is situated on the left hand side.

MAIDENHEAD UNITED FC

Founded: 1870
Former Names: None
Nickname: 'Magpies'
Ground: York Road, Maidenhead, Berks. SL6 1SF
Record Attendance: 7,920 (vs Southall in 1936)
Pitch Size: 110 × 75 yards

Colours: Black and White striped shirts, Black shorts
Telephone N°: (01628) 636314 (Club)
Ground Capacity: 4,000
Seating Capacity: 550
Web: www.pitchero.com/clubs/maidenheadunited
E-mail: social@maidenheadunitedfc.org

GENERAL INFORMATION
Car Parking: Grove Road and Town Hall car parks
Coach Parking: Grove Road and Town Hall car parks
Nearest Railway Station: Maidenhead (¼ mile)
Nearest Bus Station: Maidenhead
Club Shop: At the ground
Opening Times: Matchdays only
Telephone N°: (01628) 624739

GROUND INFORMATION
Away Supporters' Entrances & Sections:
No usual segregation

ADMISSION INFO (2020/2021 PRICES)
Adult Standing: £15.00
Adult Seating: £15.00
Concessionary Standing and Seating: £10.00
Under-16s Standing and Seating: £5.00
Note: Junior Magpies (Under-16s) are admitted free to matches in the League.
Programme Price: £2.00

DISABLED INFORMATION
Wheelchairs: Accommodated
Helpers: Admitted
Prices: Normal prices for the disabled. Free for helpers
Disabled Toilets: Available
Contact: (01628) 636314 (Bookings are not necessary)

Travelling Supporters' Information:
Routes: Exit M4 at Junction 7 and take the A4 to Maidenhead. Cross the River Thames bridge and turn left at the 2nd roundabout passing through the traffic lights. York Road is first right and the ground is approximately 300 yards along on the left.

NOTTS COUNTY FC |

Founded: 1862 (**Entered League**: 1888)
Nickname: 'The Magpies'
Ground: Meadow Lane Stadium, Nottingham, NG2 3HJ
Ground Capacity: 19,841 (All seats)
Record Attendance: 47,310 (12th March 1955)
Pitch Size: 109 × 72 yards

Colours: Black and White striped shirts, Black shorts
Telephone Nº: (0115) 952-9000
Ticket Office: (0115) 955-7210
Fax Number: (0115) 955-3994
Web Site: www.nottscountyfc.co.uk
E-mail: office@nottscountyfc.co.uk

GENERAL INFORMATION
Car Parking: Meadow Lane and Cattle Market
Coach Parking: Incinerator Road (Cattle Market Corner)
Nearest Railway Station: Nottingham (½ mile)
Nearest Bus Station: Broadmarsh Centre (Station Street)
Club Shop: At the ground
Opening Times: Mondays to Friday 9.00am – 5.00pm, Saturday Matchdays 9.00am until half-time, other Saturdays 9.00am – 1.00pm
Telephone Nº: (0115) 955-7200

GROUND INFORMATION
Away Supporters' Entrances & Sections:
Jimmy Sirrel Stand, Block Z – use Turnstiles 19-24

ADMISSION INFO (2019/2020 PRICES)
Adult Seating: £22.00
Under-18s Seating: £9.00
Ages 18 to 21 Seating: £16.00
Senior Citizen Seating: £16.00
Under-16s Seating: £7.00
Under-12s Seating: £1.00   (Under-7s admitted free)
Note: Discounted prices are available for advance purchases
Programme Price: £3.00

DISABLED INFORMATION
Wheelchairs: 34 spaces for home fans in the Derek Pavis Stand and Haydn Green Family Stand and 10 spaces for away fans in the Jimmy Sirrel Stand
Helpers: One helper admitted with each disabled fan
Prices: Normal prices apply for fans with disabilities.
Disabled Toilets: Available throughout the ground
Contact: (0115) 955-7241   (Bookings are necessary)
Beverley Markland – ticketoffice@nottscountyfc.co.uk

Travelling Supporters' Information:
Routes: From the North: Exit the M1 at Junction 26 following Nottingham signs (A610) then Melton Mowbray and Trent Bridge (A606) signs. Before the River Trent turn left into Meadow Lane; From the South: Exit the M1 at Junction 24 following signs for Nottingham (South) to Trent Bridge, cross the river and follow the one-way system to the right, then turn left and right at the traffic lights then second right into Meadow Lane; From the East: Take the A52 to West Bridgford/Trent Bridge, cross the river and follow the one-way system to the right then turn left and right at the traffic lights, then second right into Meadow Lane; From the West: Take the A52 into Nottingham following signs for Melton Mowbray and Trent Bridge. Before the River Trent turn left into Meadow Lane.

SOLIHULL MOORS FC

Photo courtesy of Jordan Martin Photography

Founded: 2007
Former Names: Formed by the merger of Solihull Borough FC and Moor Green FC in 2007
Nickname: 'The Moors'
Ground: Sportnation.bet Stadium, Damson Parkway, Solihull   B92 9EJ
Record Attendance: 3,681 (vs AFC Fylde, 2019)

Pitch Size: 114 × 76 yards
Colours: Yellow and Blue shirts with Blue shorts
Telephone Nº: (0121) 705-6770
Ground Capacity: 4,510
Seating Capacity: 2,522
Web site: www.solihullmoorsfc.co.uk
E-mail: info@solihullmoorsfc.co.uk

GENERAL INFORMATION

Car Parking: Limited number of spaces at the ground (£5.00 charge per car)
Coach Parking: At the ground
Nearest Railway Station: Birmingham International (2 miles)
Nearest Bus Station: Birmingham (5 miles)
Club Shop: At the ground
Opening Times: Monday to Friday and Saturday Matchdays 10.00am to 4.00pm (but closed on Wednesdays)
Telephone Nº: (0121) 705-6770

GROUND INFORMATION

Away Supporters' Entrances & Sections:
No usual segregation

ADMISSION INFO (2020/2021 PRICES)

Adult Standing: £16.00   (Online £15.00)
Adult Seating: £18.00   (Online £17.00)
Senior Citizen/Junior Standing: £9.00   (Online £8.00)
Senior Citizen/Junior Seating: £12.00   (Online £11.00)
Ages 12-18 Standing: £5.00   (Online £4.00)
Ages 12-18 Seating: £7.00   (Online £6.00)
Note: Under-12s are admitted free of charge when accompanied by a paying adult. Tickets are cheaper if purchased in advance online.
Programme Price: £3.00

DISABLED INFORMATION

Wheelchairs: 10 spaces in the Damson Homes Stand
Helpers: Admitted
Prices: Normal prices for fans with disabilities. Helpers free
Disabled Toilets: Available in the Damson Homes Stand
Contact: (0121) 705-6770 (Becci Fox)

Travelling Supporters' Information:
Routes: Exit the M42 at Junction 6 and take the A45 for 2 miles towards Birmingham. Turn left at the traffic lights near the Posthouse Hotel into Damson Parkway (signposted for Landrover/Damsonwood). Continue to the roundabout and come back along the other carriageway to the ground which is situated on the left after about 150 yards.

STOCKPORT COUNTY FC

Photohraph courtesy of Mike Petch – Mphotographic.co.uk

Founded: 1883
Former Names: Heaton Norris Rovers FC
Nickname: 'Hatters' 'County'
Ground: Edgeley Park, Hardcastle Road, Edgeley, Stockport   SK3 9DD
Ground Capacity: 10,841 (All seats)
Record Attendance: 27,833 (11th February 1950)
Pitch Size: 111 × 72 yards

Colours: Blue shirts and shorts
Telephone N°: (0161) 266-2700
Ticket Office: (0161) 266-2700
Ticket Office E-mail: tickets@stockportcounty.com
Web Site: www.stockportcounty.com
E-mail: info@stockportcounty.com

GENERAL INFORMATION
Car Parking: Available at the end of Castle Street in Edgeley
Coach Parking: As above
Nearest Railway Station: Stockport (5 minutes walk)
Nearest Bus Station: Mersey Square (10 minutes walk)
Club Shop: At the ground
Opening Times: Wednesdays and Thursdays 12.00pm–4.00pm and Fridays 12.00pm to 6.00pm.
Telephone N°: (0161) 266-2700

GROUND INFORMATION
Away Supporters' Entrances & Sections:
Viridor (Railway) End turnstiles and accommodation or turnstiles for Popular Side depending on the opponents

ADMISSION INFO (2020/2021 PRICES)
Adult Seating: £18.00
Senior Citizen/Student Seating: £12.00
Under-18s Seating: £5.00
Note: Children under the age of 6 are admitted free when accompanied by a paying adult.

DISABLED INFORMATION
Wheelchairs: 16 spaces in total. 10 in the Hardcastle Road Stand, 6 in the Cheadle Stand
Helpers: One helper admitted per disabled fan
Prices: Concessionary prices for disabled fans. Helpers are admitted free of charge
Disabled Toilets: Available
Contact: (0161) 266-2700   (Bookings are necessary) – info@stockportcounty.com

Travelling Supporters' Information:
Routes: From the North, South and West: Exit the M60 at Junction 1 and join the A560, following signs for Cheadle. After ¼ mile turn right into Edgeley Road and after 1 mile turn right into Caroline Street for the ground; From the East: Take the A6 or A560 into Stockport Town Centre and turn left into Greek Street. Take the 2nd exit into Mercian Way (from the roundabout) then turn left into Caroline Street – the ground is straight ahead.

SUTTON UNITED FC

Founded: 1898
Former Names: Formed by the amalgamation of Sutton Guild Rovers FC and Sutton Association FC
Nickname: 'U's'
Ground: The Borough Sports Ground, Sutton Sports Ground, Gander Green Lane, Sutton SM1 2EY
Record Attendance: 14,000 (vs Leeds United, 1970)

Colours: Amber shirts and shorts
Telephone No: (020) 8644-4440
Fax Number: (020) 8644-5120
Ground Capacity: 5,013
Seating Capacity: 765
Web site: www.suttonunited.net
E-mail: info@suttonunited.net

GENERAL INFORMATION

Car Parking: 150 spaces behind the Main Stand for permit holders only. Otherwise, street parking is usually possible
Coach Parking: Space for 1 coach in the car park
Nearest Railway Station: West Sutton (adjacent)
Club Shop: At the ground
Opening Times: Matchdays only
Telephone No: (020) 8644-4440

GROUND INFORMATION

Away Supporters' Entrances & Sections:
Collingwood Road entrances and accommodation

ADMISSION INFO (2020/2021 PRICES)

Adult Standing/Seating: £17.00
Concessionary Standing/Seating: £10.00
Junior Standing/Seating: £5.00
Note: Under-11s are admitted free of charge
Programme Price: £3.00

DISABLED INFORMATION

Wheelchairs: 8 spaces are available under cover accommodated on the track perimeter
Helpers: Admitted
Prices: Normal prices apply for the disabled. Free for helpers
Disabled Toilets: Available alongside the Standing Terrace
Contact: (020) 8644-4440 (Bookings are necessary) – Mike Chenery (Disability Liaison Officer) 07974 808749 or e-mail mike.chenery@suttonunited.net

Travelling Supporters' Information:
Routes: Exit the M25 at Junction 8 (Reigate Hill) and travel North on the A217 for approximately 8 miles. Cross the A232 then turn right at the traffic lights (past Goose & Granit Public House) into Gander Green Lane. The ground is 300 yards on the left; From London: Gander Green Lane crosses the Sutton bypass 1 mile south of Rose Hill Roundabout. Avoid Sutton Town Centre, especially on Saturdays.

TORQUAY UNITED FC

Founded: 1899
Former Name: Torquay Town FC (1899-1910)
Nickname: 'Gulls'
Ground: Plainmoor Ground, Torquay   TQ1 3PS
Ground Capacity: 6,200   **Seating Capacity**: 2,841
Record Attendance: 21,908 (29th January 1955)
Pitch Size: 112 × 72 yards

Colours: Yellow shirts and Blue shorts
Telephone Nº: (01803) 328666
Ticket Office: (01803) 328666
Fax Number: (01803) 323976
Web Site: www.torquayunited.com
E-mail: reception@torquayunited.com

GENERAL INFORMATION
Car Parking: Street parking
Coach Parking: Lymington Road Coach Station (½ mile)
Nearest Railway Station: Torre (1¼ miles) or Torquay (2 miles)
Nearest Bus Station: Lymington Road (½ mile)
Club Shop: At the ground
Opening Times: Monday to Friday 10.00am to 4.30pm, Tuesday Matchdays 10.00am until kick-off then until after the final whistle until 10.00pm. Saturday Matchdays 12.00pm to 3.00pm then until 5.30pm following the final whistle.
Telephone Nº: (01803) 328666

GROUND INFORMATION
Away Supporters' Entrances & Sections:
Riviera Rentals away terrace

ADMISSION INFO (2020/2021 PRICES)
Adult Standing: £16.00
Adult Seating: £17.00 – £18.00
Concessionary Standing: £14.00
Concessionary Seating: £15.00 – £16.00
Under-18s Standing/Seating: £10.00
Note: Under-7s are admitted free with a paying adult and Family tickets are also available.
Programme Price: £3.00

DISABLED INFORMATION
Wheelchairs: Spaces for both Home and Away fans are available in front of Bristow Bench Stand.
Helpers: One helper admitted per wheelchair
Prices: Normal prices for the disabled. Free for helpers
Disabled Toilets: In the Ellacombe End and the Away End
Contact: (01803) 328666   (Bookings are not necessary) Jo Harris (Liaison Officer) – joanneh@torquayunited.com

Travelling Supporters' Information:
Routes: From the North and East: Take the M5 to the A38 then A380 to Torquay. On entering Torquay, turn left at the 1st set of traffic lights after Riviera Way Retail Park into Hele Road. Following signs for the ground, continue straight on over two mini-roundabouts, go up West Hill Road to the traffic lights, then straight ahead into Warbro Road. The ground is situated on the right after 200 yards.

WEALDSTONE FC

Founded: 1899
Former Names: None
Nickname: 'The Stones' or 'The Royals'
Ground: Grosvenor Vale, Ruislip   HA4 6JQ
Record Attendance: 2,469 (vs Colchester Utd, 2015)
Colours: Royal Blue shirts with White shorts

Contact Telephone Nº: 07790 038095 (Paul Fruin – Club Secretary)
Ground Capacity: 3,607
Seating Capacity: 709
Web site: www.wealdstone-fc.com
E-mail: wealdstonefc@btinternet.com

GENERAL INFORMATION

Car Parking: 100 spaces available at the ground
Coach Parking: Available outside the ground
Nearest Mainline Station: West Ruislip (1 mile)
Nearest Tube Station: Ruislip (½ mile)
Club Shop: At the ground
Opening Times: Matchdays only plus online sales
Telephone Nº: –

GROUND INFORMATION

Away Supporters' Entrances & Sections:
No usual segregation

ADMISSION INFO (2020/2021 PRICES)

Adult Standing/Seating: £15.00
Concessionary Standing/Seating: £10.00
Under-18s Standing/Seating: £5.00
Note: Under-14s are admitted free of charge when accompanied by a paying adult
Programme Price: £3.00

DISABLED INFORMATION

Wheelchairs: Accommodated
Helpers: Admitted
Prices: Concessionary prices apply for disabled fans
Disabled Toilets: Available
Contact: (01895) 637487

Travelling Supporters' Information:
Routes: Exit the M25 at Junction 16 and take the A40 towards Uxbridge. At the Polish War Memorial Junction with the A4180, follow the Ruislip signs (West End Road). After about 1½ miles, turn right into Grosvenor Vale for the ground.

WEYMOUTH FC

Founded: 1890
Former Names: None
Nickname: 'Terras'
Ground: Bob Lucas Stadium, Radipole Lane, Weymouth, Dorset DT4 9XJ
Ground Capacity: 6,600   **Seating Capacity**: 900
Record Attendance: 6,500 (14th November 2005)

Colours: Sky Blue shirts with Claret trim, Blue shorts
Telephone Nº: (01305) 785558
Web site: www.theterras.com
E-mail: info@theterras.com

GENERAL INFORMATION

Car Parking: 200 spaces available at the ground
Coach Parking: At the ground
Nearest Railway Station: Weymouth (2 miles)
Nearest Bus Station: Weymouth Town Centre
Club Shop: At the ground
Opening Times: Matchdays only
Telephone Nº: (01305) 785558

GROUND INFORMATION

Away Supporters' Entrances & Sections:
No usual segregation

ADMISSION INFO (2020/2021 PRICES)

Adult Standing/Seating: £16.00
Concessionary Standing/Seating: £11.00
Under-19s Standing/Seating: £7.00
Under-16s Standing/Seating: £4.00
Under-7s Standing/Seating: 50p

DISABLED INFORMATION

Wheelchairs: Accommodated pitchside in front of the Main Stand
Helpers: Admitted
Prices: Concessionary prices apply for the disabled. Helpers are admitted free of charge
Disabled Toilets: Available adjacent to the wheelchair area
Contact: (01305) 785558   (Bookings are not necessary)

Travelling Supporters' Information:
Routes: Take the A354 from Dorchester to Weymouth and turn right at the first roundabout to the town centre. Take the 3rd exit at the next roundabout and follow signs for the ground which is about ½ mile on the right.

WOKING FC

Founded: 1889
Former Names: None
Nickname: 'Cardinals'
Ground: Laithwaite Community Stadium, Kingfield, Woking, Surrey   GU22 9AA
Record Attendance: 6,064 (vs Coventry City, 1997)
Pitch Size: 109 × 76 yards

Colours: Shirts are Red & White halves, Black shorts
Telephone N°: (01483) 772470
Fax Number: (01483) 888423
Ground Capacity: 6,161
Seating Capacity: 2,511
Web site: www.wokingfc.co.uk
E-mail: admin@wokingfc.co.uk

GENERAL INFORMATION

Car Parking: Limited parking at the ground
Coach Parking: Please contact the club for details
Nearest Railway Station: Woking (1 mile)
Nearest Bus Station: Woking
Club Shop: At the ground
Opening Times: Tuesdays 1.00pm to 5.00pm, Thursdays 9.00am to 1.00pm and Matchdays
Telephone N°: (01483) 772470 Extension 240

GROUND INFORMATION

Away Supporters' Entrances & Sections:
Kingfield Road entrance for the Chris Lane terrace

ADMISSION INFO (2019/2020 PRICES)

Adult Standing: £18.00
Adult Seating: £18.00
Under-16s/Student Standing: £5.00
Under-16s/Student Seating: £5.00
Senior Citizen Standing: £13.00
Senior Citizen Seating: £13.00

DISABLED INFORMATION

Wheelchairs: 8 spaces in the Leslie Gosden Stand and 8 spaces in front of the Family Stand
Helpers: Admitted
Prices: Concessionary prices apply for disabled fans. Helpers are admitted free of charge
Disabled Toilets: Yes – in the Leslie Gosden Stand and Family Stand area
Contact: (01483) 772470   (Bookings are necessary)

Travelling Supporters' Information:
Routes: Exit the M25 at Junction 10 and follow the A3 towards Guildford. Leave at the next junction onto the B2215 through Ripley and join the A247 to Woking. Alternatively, exit the M25 at Junction 11 and follow the A320 to Woking Town Centre. The ground is on the outskirts of Woking – follow signs on the A320 and A247.

WREXHAM AFC

Founded: 1864
Nickname: 'Red Dragons'
Ground: Racecourse Ground, Mold Road, Wrexham, North Wales LL11 2AH
Ground Capacity: 10,500 (all seats)
Record Attendance: 34,445 (26th January 1957)
Pitch Size: 111 × 74 yards

Colours: Red shirts with White shorts
Telephone N°: (01978) 891864
Web Site: www.wrexhamafc.co.uk
E-mail: info@wrexhamfc.tv

GENERAL INFORMATION

Car Parking: Town car parks are nearby and also Glyndwr University (Mold End)
Coach Parking: By Police direction
Nearest Railway Station: Wrexham General (adjacent)
Nearest Bus Station: Wrexham (King Street)
Club Shop: At the ground under the bkoncepts Stand
Opening Times: Monday to Friday 10.00am to 5.00pm and home Matchdays 10.00am until kick-off.
Telephone N°: (01978) 891864

GROUND INFORMATION

Away Supporters' Entrances & Sections:
Turnstiles 1-4 for the bkoncepts Stand

ADMISSION INFO (2019/2020 PRICES)

Adult Seating: £16.00 – £20.00
Concession Seniors/Under-21s Seating: £13.00–£15.00
Concession Over-80s/Under-18s Seating: £7.00 – £8.00
Under-11s Seating: £1.00 (with a paying adult)
Note: Discounts apply for advance purchases and Family tickets are also available

DISABLED INFORMATION

Wheelchairs: 35 spaces in the Mold Road Stand
Helpers: One helper admitted per wheelchair
Prices: Normal prices for the disabled. Free for helpers
Disabled Toilets: Available in the disabled section
Contact: (01978) 891864 – Dan Sear (Liaison Officer) – ticketoffice@wrexhamfc.tv

Travelling Supporters' Information:
Routes: From the North and West: Take the A483 and the Wrexham bypass to the junction with the A541. Branch left at the roundabout and follow Wrexham signs into Mold Road; From the East: Take the A525 or A534 into Wrexham then follow the A541 signs into Mold Road; From the South: Take the the M6, then the M54 and follow the A5 and A483 to the Wrexham bypass and the junction with the A541. Branch right at the roundabout and follow signs for the Town Centre.

YEOVIL TOWN FC

Founded: 1895
Former Names: Yeovil & Petters United FC
Nickname: 'Glovers'
Ground: Huish Park Stadium, Lufton Way, Yeovil, Somerset BA22 8YF
Ground Capacity: 9,565 **Seating Capacity**: 5,309
Record Attendance: 9,527 (25th April 2008)

Pitch Size: 108 × 67 yards
Colours: Green and White shirts with White shorts
Telephone Nº: (01935) 423662
Ticket Office Nº: (01935) 847888
Fax Number: (01935) 473956
Web site: www.ytfc.net
E-mail: info@ytfc.net

GENERAL INFORMATION

Car Parking: Spaces for 800 cars at the ground (£3.00)
Coach Parking: At the ground
Nearest Railway Station: Yeovil Pen Mill (2½ miles) and Yeovil Junction (3½ miles)
Nearest Bus Station: Yeovil (2 miles)
Club Shop: At the ground
Opening Times: Weekdays 10.00am – 4.00pm and Matchdays 10.00am – 3.00pm
Telephone Nº: (01935) 423662

GROUND INFORMATION

Away Supporters' Entrances & Sections:
Away Terrace (turnstiles 13-16) and Screwfix Community Stand (turnstile 12)

ADMISSION INFO (2020/2021 PRICES)

Adult Standing: £16.00
Adult Seating: £19.00
Under-16s Standing/Seating: £3.00
Ages 16 to 22 Standing/Seating: £12.00
Senior Citizen/Armed Forces Standing: £14.00
Senior Citizen/Armed Forces Seating: £17.00
Note: Discounted prices are available for tickets which are purchased before the day of the match.

DISABLED INFORMATION

Wheelchairs: 15 spaces for home fans, 5 spaces for away fans
Helpers: Admitted free of charge
Prices: Concessionary prices apply for disabled fans
Disabled Toilets: Two are available
Contact: (01935) 423662 or 07779 261814 (Bookings are recommended). James Hillier (Liaison Officer) – jhillier@ytfc.net

Travelling Supporters' Information:
Routes: From London: Take the M3 and A303 to Cartgate Roundabout. Enter Yeovil on the A3088. Exit left at the 1st roundabout then straight over the next two roundabouts into Western Avenue. Cross the next roundabout then turn left into Copse Road, where supporters' parking is sited; From the North: Exit the M5 at Junction 25 and take the A358 (Ilminster) and A303 (Eastbound) entering Yeovil on the A3088. Then as above.

THE VANARAMA NATIONAL LEAGUE NORTH

Address

4th Floor, 20 Waterloo Street,
Birmingham   B2 5TB

Phone (0121) 643-3143

Web site   www.footballconference.co.uk

Clubs for the 2020/2021 Season

AFC FYLDE

Photo courtesy of John Mills @ Altius Photography

Founded: 1988
Former Names: Formed by the amalgamation of Wesham FC and Kirkham Town FC in 1988
Nickname: 'The Coasters'
Ground: Mill Farm, Coronation Way, Wesham, Preston   PR4 3JZ
Record Attendance: 3,858   (26th December 2016)

Colours: White shirts and shorts
Telephone Nº: (01772) 682593
Ground Capacity: 6,000
Seating Capacity: 2,000
Pitch Size: 110 × 72 yards
Web Site: www.afcfylde.co.uk
E-mail: info@afcfylde.co.uk

GENERAL INFORMATION

Car Parking: A limited number of spaces are available at the ground (£5.00 charge) and there also is an overflow parking facility nearby.
Coach Parking: At the ground
Nearest Railway Station: Kirkham & Wesham (1 mile)
Club Shop: At the ground
Opening Times: Monday to Saturday 9.00am to 5.00pm. Tuesday Matchdays 10.00am to 10.00pm and Saturday Matchdays 9.00am to 6.00pm
Telephone Nº: (01772) 682593 (Phone orders accepted)

GROUND INFORMATION

Away Supporters' Entrances & Sections:
South Terrace standing and Seating in Block A.

ADMISSION INFO (2019/2020 PRICES)

Adult Standing: £14.00
Adult Seating: £18.00
Ages 16 to 21 Standing: £8.00
Under-16s Seating: £10.00
Under-16s Standing: £6.00
Note: Discounted prices are available for members.
Programme Price: £3.00

DISABLED INFORMATION

Wheelchairs: Accommodated
Helpers: Admitted
Prices: Normal prices apply for the disabled. One helper is admitted free of charge with each paying disabled fan.
Disabled Toilets: Available
Contact: (01772) 682593   (Bookings are necessary)

Travelling Supporters' Information:
Routes: The Mill Farm Sports Village is situated by the side of the A585, just to the north of Wesham and less than a mile to the south of Junction 3 of the M55.

AFC TELFORD UNITED

Founded: 2004
Former Names: Formed after Telford United FC went out of business. TUFC were previously known as Wellington Town FC
Nickname: 'The Bucks'
Ground: The New Bucks Head Stadium, Watling Street, Wellington, Telford TF1 2TU
Record Attendance: 13,000 (1935 vs Shrewsbury T.)

Pitch Size: 110 × 74 yards
Colours: White shirts with Black shorts
Telehone Nº: (01952) 640064
Ground Capacity: 6,300
Seating Capacity: 2,200
Web site: www.telfordunited.com
E-mail: enquiries@afctu.co.uk

GENERAL INFORMATION
Car Parking: At the ground (£3.00 charge for cars)
Coach Parking: At the ground
Nearest Railway Station: Wellington
Nearest Bus Station: Wellington
Club Shop: At the ground
Opening Times: Saturday matchdays only from 1.30pm.
Telephone Nº: (01952) 640064

GROUND INFORMATION
Away Supporters' Entrances & Sections:
Frank Nagington Stand on the rare occasions when segregation is used

ADMISSION INFO (2019/2020 PRICES)
Adult Standing: £14.00
Adult Seating: £14.00
Under-16s Standing: £1.00
Under-16s Seating: £1.00
Under-20s Standing: £5.00
Under-20s Seating: £5.00
Concessionary Standing: £8.00
Concessionary Seating: £8.00

DISABLED INFORMATION
Wheelchairs: Accommodated at both ends of the ground
Helpers: Admitted
Prices: Concessionary prices apply for disabled supporters. Helpers are admitted free of charge
Disabled Toilets: Available by the Sir Stephen Roberts Stand
Contact: (01952) 640064   (Bookings are not necessary)

Travelling Supporters' Information:
Routes: Exit the M54 at Junction 6 and take the A518. Go straight on at the first roundabout, take the second exit at the next roundabout then turn left at the following roundabout. Follow the road round to the right then turn left into the car park.

ALFRETON TOWN FC

Founded: 1959
Former Names: None
Nickname: 'Reds'
Ground: The Impact Arena, North Street, Alfreton, Derbyshire   DE55 7FZ
Record Attendance: 5,023 vs Matlock Town (1960)
Pitch Size: 110 × 75 yards

Colours: Red shirts and shorts
Telephone Nº: (01773) 830277
Ground Capacity: 3,600
Seating Capacity: 1,500
Web site: www.alfretontownfootballclub.com
E-mail: enquiries@alfretontownfootballclub.com

GENERAL INFORMATION

Car Parking: At the ground plus street parking
Coach Parking: Available close to the ground
Nearest Railway Station: Alfreton (½ mile)
Nearest Bus Station: Alfreton (5 minutes walk)
Club Shop: At the ground
Opening Times: Weekdays 9.00am to 3.00pm
Telephone Nº: (01773) 830277

GROUND INFORMATION

Away Supporters' Entrances & Sections:
'Tin End' terrace behind the North Street goal

ADMISSION INFO (2019/2020 PRICES)

Adult Standing: £14.00
Adult Seating: £14.00
Senior Citizen Standing/Seating: £10.00
Ages 16 to 21 Standing/Seating: £10.00
Under-16s Standing: £2.00 (with a paying adult)
Under-16s Seating: £2.00 (with a paying adult)

DISABLED INFORMATION

Wheelchairs: Accommodated in dedicated areas of the ground
Helpers: Admitted
Prices: Normal prices for disabled fans. Free for helpers
Disabled Toilets: Available in Zones 3 and 8
Contact: (01773) 830277   (Bookings are not necessary)

Travelling Supporters' Information:
Routes: Exit the M1 at Junction 28 and take the A38 signposted for Derby. After 2 miles take the sliproad onto the B600 then go right at the main road towards the town centre. After ½ mile turn left down North Street and the ground is on the right after 200 yards.

BLYTH SPARTANS AFC

Founded: 1899
Former Names: None
Nickname: 'Spartans'
Ground: Croft Park, Blyth, Northumberland, NE24 3JE
Record Attendance: 10,186 (1956)
Pitch Size: 110 × 70 yards

Colours: Green and White striped shirts, Black shorts
Telephone Nº: (01670) 352373 (Office)
Ground Capacity: 4,435
Seating Capacity: 556
Web site: www.blythspartans.com
E-mail: generalmanager@blythspartans.com

GENERAL INFORMATION
Car Parking: At the ground
Coach Parking: At the ground
Nearest Railway Station: Newcastle
Nearest Bus Station: Blyth (5 minutes walk)
Club Shop: At the ground
Opening Times: Matchdays only
Telephone Nº: (01670) 352373

GROUND INFORMATION
Away Supporters' Entrances & Sections:
No usual segregation

ADMISSION INFO (2020/2021 PRICES)
Adult Standing: £12.00   **Adult Seating**: £14.00
Senior Citizen Standing: £7.00
Senior Citizen Seating: £9.00
Ages 11 to 16 & Student Standing: £5.00
Ages 11 to 16 & Student Seating: £7.00
Note: Under-11s are admitted free of charge when accompanied by a paying adult
Programme Price: £2.00

DISABLED INFORMATION
Wheelchairs: 3 elevated wheelchair spaces available
Helpers: Please phone the club for information
Prices: Adult disabled fans are charged the Senior Citizen rate shown above. Younger disabled fans charged lower rate.
Disabled Toilets: Available adjacent to the Main Stand
Contact: (01670) 352373 (Bookings are necessary)

Travelling Supporters' Information:
Routes: Pass through the Tyne Tunnel and take the left lane for Morpeth (A19/A1). At the 2nd roundabout (after approximately 7 miles) take full right turn for the A189 (signposted Ashington). After 2 miles take the slip road (A1061 signposted Blyth). Follow signs for Blyth turning left at the caravan site. At the 2nd roundabout turn right and the ground is on the left.

BOSTON UNITED FC

At the time of going to press, no image was available for the Jakemans Community Stadium, so the image above shows the club's old ground, York Street.

Founded: 1933
Former Names: Boston Town FC & Boston Swifts FC
Nickname: 'The Pilgrims'
Ground: The Jakemans Community Stadium, Pilgrim Way, Wyberton, Boston   PE21 7NE
Ground Capacity: 5,000   **Seating Capacity**: 2,400
Pitch Size: 112 × 72 yards
Record Attendance: 11,000   (vs Derby County, 1974)

Colours: Amber and Black shirts, Black shorts
Telephone Nº: (01205) 364406   (Office)
Matchday Info: (01205) 364406
Web Site: www.bostonunited.co.uk
E-mail: admin@bufc.co.uk

GENERAL INFORMATION

Car Parking: At the ground
Coach Parking: At the ground
Nearest Railway Station: Boston   (1 mile)
Nearest Bus Station: Boston Coach Station
Club Shop: At the ground
Opening Times: Weekdays and Saturday Matchdays from 9.00am to 5.00pm
Telephone Nº: (01205) 364406

GROUND INFORMATION

Away Supporters' Entrances & Sections:
Accommodation in the Main Stand for matches where segregation is in force

ADMISSION INFO (2020/2021 PRICES)

Adult Standing: £13.00
Adult Seating: £15.00
Child Standing: £4.00
Child Seating: £5.00
Senior Citizen Standing: £10.00
Senior Citizen Seating: £11.00
Note: Discounted family tickets may be available. Please contact the club for further information.

DISABLED INFORMATION

Wheelchairs: Accommodated in the Main Stand
Helpers: One helper admitted per disabled fan
Prices: £10.00 for disabled fans using wheelchairs. Free of charge for helpers
Disabled Toilets: Available
Contact: (01205) 364406   (Bookings are necessary)

Travelling Supporters' Information:
The Jakemans Community Stadium is located by the side of the A16 on the outskirts of Wyberton which is just to the south of Boston. The Stadium is clearly signposted from the A16.

BRACKLEY TOWN FC

Founded: 1890
Former Names: None
Nickname: 'Saints'
Ground: St. James Park, Churchill Way, Brackley, NN13 7EJ
Record Attendance: 2,604 (12th May 2013)

Colours: Red and White shirts with White shorts
Telephone N°: (01280) 704077
Ground Capacity: 3,500
Seating Capacity: 300
Web Site: www.brackleytownfc.com
E-mail: janenebutters@brackleytownfc.co.uk

GENERAL INFORMATION

Car Parking: At the ground (£2.00 charge per car)
Coach Parking: At the ground
Nearest Railway Station: King's Sutton (6¾ miles)
Club Shop: At the ground
Opening Times: Matchdays and by appointment only
Telephone N°: (01280) 704077

GROUND INFORMATION

Away Supporters' Entrances & Sections:
Accommodation in the Cricket Ground end for games when segregation is in force

ADMISSION INFO (2020/2021 PRICES)

Adult Standing: £13.00
Adult Seating: £13.00
Senior Citizen/Student Standing: £8.00
Senior Citizen/Student Seating: £8.00
Under-18s Standing: £5.00
Under-18s Seating: £5.00
Under-10s Seating/Standing: £1.00

DISABLED INFORMATION

Wheelchairs: Accommodated
Helpers: Admitted
Prices: Normal prices apply for the disabled. Free for helpers
Disabled Toilets: Available
Contact: (01280) 704077 (Bookings are necessary)

Travelling Supporters' Information:
Routes: From the West: Take the A422 to Brackley and take the first exit at the roundabout with the junction of the A43, heading north into Oxford Road.* Go straight on at the next roundabout and continue into Bridge Street before turning right into Churchill Way. The ground is located at the end of the road; From the South: Take the A43 northwards to Brackley. Take the second exit at the roundabout with the junction of the A422 and head into Oxford Road. Then as from * above; From the North-East: Take the A43 to Brackley. Upon reaching Brackley, take the 1st exit at the 1st roundabout, the 2nd exit at the next roundabout then the 3rd exit at the following roundabout into Oxford Road. Then as from * above.

BRADFORD PARK AVENUE FC

Founded: 1907   (Re-formed in 1988)
Former Names: None
Nickname: 'Avenue'
Ground: Horsfall Stadium, Cemetery Road, Bradford, BD6 2NG
Ground Capacity: 3,500   **Seating Capacity**: 1,800
Record Attendance: 2,100 (2003)
Pitch Size: 112 × 71 yards

Colours: Red, Yellow and Black hooped shirts with Black shorts and socks
Telephone Nº: (01274) 674584
Web site: www.bpafc.com
E-mail: info@bpafc.com

GENERAL INFORMATION
Car Parking: Street parking and some spaces at the ground
Coach Parking: At the ground
Nearest Railway Station: Bradford Interchange (3 miles)
Nearest Bus Station: Bradford Interchange (3 miles)
Club Shop: At the ground
Opening Times: Matchdays only
Telephone Nº: (01274) 674584

GROUND INFORMATION
Away Supporters' Entrances & Sections:
Segregation only used when required

ADMISSION INFO (2020/2021 PRICES)
Adult Standing/Seating: £14.00
Senior Citizen Standing/Seating: £10.00
Student Standing/Seating: £5.00
Under-16s Standing/Seating: £3.00
Under-11s Standing/Seating: £1.00 when accompanying a paying adult

DISABLED INFORMATION
Wheelchairs: Accommodated in front of the Stand
Helpers: Admitted
Prices: Normal prices for disabled fans. Helpers free of charge
Disabled Toilets: Available in the clubhouse
Contact: (01274) 674584   (Bookings are not necessary)

Travelling Supporters' Information:
Routes: Exit the M62 at Junction 26 and take the M606 to its end. At the roundabout go along the A6036 (signposted Halifax) and pass Odsal Stadium on the left. At the roundabout by Odsal take the 3rd exit (still A6036 Halifax). After just under 1 mile, turn left at the Kinderhaven Nursery into Cemetery Road. The ground is 150 yards on the left.

CHESTER FC

Founded: 1885
Former Names: Chester FC and Chester City FC
Nickname: 'Blues'
Ground: Swansway Chester Stadium, Bumpers Lane, Chester CH1 4LT
Pitch Size: 116 × 75 yards
Record Attendance: 5,987 (17th April 2004)

Colours: Blue and White striped shirts, White shorts
Ground Telephone N°: (01244) 371376
Ticket Office: (01244) 371376
Ground Capacity: 6,500
Seating Capacity: 4,170
Web site: www.chesterfc.com
E-mail: info@chesterfc.com

GENERAL INFORMATION

Car Parking: Ample spaces available at the ground (£2.00)
Coach Parking: Available at the ground
Nearest Railway Station: Chester (2 miles)
Nearest Bus Station: Chester (1½ miles)
Club Shop: At the ground
Opening Times: Weekdays & matchdays 10.00am–4.00pm
Telephone N°: (01244) 371376

GROUND INFORMATION

Away Supporters' Entrances & Sections:
South Stand for covered seating and also part of the West Stand

ADMISSION INFO (2020/2021 PRICES)

Adult Standing: £14.00   **Adult Seating**: £17.00
Concessionary Standing: £12.00   **Seating**: £14.00
Ages 18 to 21 Standing: £10.00   **Seating**: £12.00
Ages 12 to 17 Seating/Standing: £3.00
Under-12s: Free of charge

DISABLED INFORMATION

Wheelchairs: 40 spaces for wheelchairs in the West Stand and East Stand
Helpers: Admitted
Prices: Normal prices for the disabled. Free for helpers
Disabled Toilets: Available in West and East Stands
Contact: (01244) 371376 (Bookings are necessary)
Bob Marsden (Liaison) – bobbymarsden259@gmail.com

Travelling Supporters' Information:
Routes: From the North: Take the M56, A41 or A56 into the Town Centre and then follow Queensferry (A548) signs into Sealand Road. Turn left at the traffic lights by 'Tesco' into Bumpers Lane – the ground is ½ mile at the end of the road; From the East: Take the A54 or A51 into the Town Centre (then as North); From the South: Take the A41 or A483 into Town Centre (then as North); From the West: Take the A55, A494 or A548 and follow Queensferry signs towards Birkenhead (A494) and after 1¼ miles bear left onto the A548 (then as North); From the M6/M56 (Avoiding Town Centre): Take the M56 to Junction 16 (signposted Queensferry), turn left at the roundabout onto A5117, signposted Wales. At the next roundabout turn left onto the A5480 (signposted Chester) and after approximately 3 miles take the 3rd exit from the roundabout (signposted Sealand Road Industrial Parks). Go straight across 2 sets of traffic lights into Bumpers Lane. The ground is ½ mile on the right.

CHORLEY FC

Founded: 1883
Former Names: None
Nickname: 'Magpies'
Ground: The Chorley Group Victory Park Stadium, Duke Street, Chorley, PR7 3DU
Record Attendance: 9,679 (v Darwen 15/11/1932)
Pitch Size: 112 × 72 yards

Colours: Black & White striped shirts with Black shorts
Telephone N°: (01257) 230007
Ground Capacity: 4,100
Seating Capacity: 980
Web site: www.chorleyfc.com
E-mail: commercial@chorleyfc.com

GENERAL INFORMATION
Car Parking: Pilling Lane (£3.00)
Coach Parking: At the ground
Nearest Railway Station: Chorley (¼ mile)
Nearest Bus Station: 15 minutes from the ground
Club Shop: At the ground
Opening Times: Weekdays 12.00pm to 2.00pm and Matchdays 12.00pm until kick-off.
Telephone N°: (01257) 230007

GROUND INFORMATION
Away Supporters' Entrances & Sections:
Pilling Lane Stand entrances and accommodation

ADMISSION INFO (2020/2021 PRICES)
Adult Standing: £15.00
Adult Seating: £15.00
Concessionary Standing/Seating: £12.00
Ages 18 to 21 Standing/Seating: £7.00
Ages 12 to 17 Standing/Seating: £5.00
Under-12s Standing/Seating: Free of charge but must be accompanied by an adult
Programme Price: £2.50

DISABLED INFORMATION
Wheelchairs: Accommodated by prior arrangement
Helpers: Admitted
Prices: Normal prices for disabled fans. Helpers free of charge
Disabled Toilets: Available in the Social Club
Contact: (01257) 230007   (Bookings are not necessary)

Travelling Supporters' Information:
Routes: Exit the M61 at Junction 6 and follow the A6 to Chorley. Going past the Yarrow Bridge Hotel on Bolton Road, turn left at the 1st set of traffic lights into Pilling Lane. Take the 1st right into Ashby Street and the ground is the 2nd entrance on the left; Alternative Route: Exit the M6 at Junction 27 and follow signs to Chorley. Turn left at the lights and continue down the A49 for 2½ miles before turning right onto B5251. On entering Chorley, turn right into Duke Street 200 yards past The Plough.

CURZON ASHTON FC

Founded: 1963
Former Names: None
Nickname: 'The Nash'
Ground: Tameside Stadium, Richmond Street, Ashton-under-Lyne OL7 9HG
Record Attendance: 3,210 (2007)
Pitch Size: 114 × 72 yards

Colours: Royal Blue shirts and shorts
Telephone Nº: (0161) 330-6033
Ground Capacity: 4,000
Seating Capacity: 527
Web Site: www.curzon-ashton.co.uk
E-mail: rob@curzon-ashton.co.uk

GENERAL INFORMATION
Car Parking: At the ground
Coach Parking: At the ground
Nearest Railway Station: Ashton-under-Lyne (1 mile)
Club Shop: At the ground
Opening Times: Matchdays only
Telephone Nº: (0161) 330-6033

GROUND INFORMATION
Away Supporters' Entrances & Sections:
No usual segregation

ADMISSION INFO (2020/2021 PRICES)
Adult Standing/Seating: £14.00
Senior Citizen Standing/Seating: £7.00
Under-16s Standing/Seating: £3.00
Student Standing/Seating: The club offer Students 'Pay What You Can Afford' admission with a minimum charge of £3.00 applied.
Programme Price: £2.00

DISABLED INFORMATION
Wheelchairs: Accommodated
Helpers: Admitted
Prices: Normal prices apply for the disabled and helpers
Disabled Toilets: Available
Contact: (0161) 330-6033 (Bookings are not necessary)

Travelling Supporters' Information:
Routes: Exit the M60 at Junction 23 and take the A6140 signposted for Ashton. Continue along the A6140 to the set of traffic lights with a Cinema on the right then turn left. Cross over a bridge and go straight across the mini-roundabout before turning left into the ground.

DARLINGTON FC

Founded: 1883 (Re-formed 2012)
Former Names: Successor to the club Darlington FC, formed as Darlington 1883 and renamed in 2017
Nickname: 'Darlo', 'The Quakers'
Ground: Blackwell Meadows, Grange Road, Darlington   DL1 5NR
Record Attendance: 3,000 (26th December 2016)
Pitch Size: 110 × 75 yards

Ground Capacity: 3,100
Seating Capacity: 588
Colours: Black and White hooped shirts, Black shorts
Contact Telephone Nº: None
Web Site: www.darlingtonfc.co.uk
E-mail: dave.watson@darlingtonfc.org

GENERAL INFORMATION

Car Parking: A limited number of spaces at Blackwell Meadows are available on a first-come, first-served basis with a £5.00 fee. Alternatively, use town centre car parks (1½ miles)
Coach Parking: Limited parking at the ground
Nearest Railway Station: Darlington (1½ miles)
Nearest Bus Station: Darlington Town Centre (1½ miles)
Club Shop: Quaker Retail at the Dolphin Centre, Darlington and at Mysportswear, Morton Park, Darlington
Opening Times: Weekdays 10.00am to 1.00pm.
Telephone Nº: 07488 564642 (Quaker Retail) and (01325) 488884 (Mysportswear)

GROUND INFORMATION

Away Supporters' Entrances & Sections:
Western End of the ground when segregation is in force

ADMISSION INFO (2020/2021 PRICES)

Adult Standing: £14.00
Adult Seating: £16.00
Concessionary Standing: £10.00
Concessionary Seating: £12.00
Under-16s Standing: £5.00
Under-16s Seating: £7.00
Under-11s Standing/Seating: Free of charge when accompanied by a paying adult
Note: Tickets are cheaper if purchased in advance online.
Programme Price: £2.50

DISABLED INFORMATION

Wheelchairs: Accommodated
Helpers: Helpers are admitted
Prices: Concessionary prices for the disabled and helpers
Disabled Toilets: Available
Contact: dave.watson@darlingtonfc.org   (Bookings are necessary)

Travelling Supporters' Information:
Routes: From the South: Exit the A1(M) at Junction 57 and take the A66(M) towards Darlington. At the end of the motorway, continue onto the A66 and take the second exit at the next roundabout onto the A167 Darlington Road. Blackwell Meadows is on the right after 400 yards; From the North: Exit the A1(M) at Junction 59 and take the A167 to Darlington. Upon entering Darlington, continue along the A167, taking the second exit at the roundabout into North Road, the first exit at Northgate Roundabout onto St. Cuthbert's Way then following the road around around Darlington town centre into Victoria Road before turning left at the Baptist church into Grange Road. Blackwell Meadows in on the left after approximately 1 mile.

FARSLEY CELTIC AFC

Founded: 1908 (Original club)
Former Names: Farsley Celtic FC
Nickname: 'Villagers'
Ground: The Citadel, Newlands, Farsley, Leeds, LS28 5BE
Record Attendance: 2,462 (2006)
Pitch Size: 110 × 67 yards

Colours: White and Green hooped shirts with Green shorts
Telephone Nº: 07736 034604 or 07725 999758
Ground Capacity: 4,000
Seating Capacity: 300
Web site: www.farsleyceltic.com
E-mail: office@farsleyceltic.com

GENERAL INFORMATION

Car Parking: Available at the ground
Coach Parking: Available at the ground
Nearest Railway Station: New Pudsey (1 mile)
Nearest Bus Station: Pudsey (1 mile)
Club Shop: At the ground
Opening Times: Weekday evenings 6.00pm – 11.00pm and weekends noon until 11.00pm
Telephone Nº: 07736 037604

GROUND INFORMATION

Away Supporters' Entrances & Sections:
No usual segregation

ADMISSION INFO (2020/2021 PRICES)

Adult Standing: £12.00
Adult Seating: £12.00
Senior Citizen/Student/Under-18s Standing: £7.00
Senior Citizen/Student/Under-18s Seating: £7.00
Under-13s/Armed Forces/Emergency Services: Free
Programme Price: £2.00

DISABLED INFORMATION

Wheelchairs: Accommodated
Helpers: Please phone the club for information
Prices: Please phone the club for information
Disabled Toilets: Available
Contact: 07736 037604 (Bookings are necessary)

Travelling Supporters' Information:
Routes: From the North: Take the A1 to Wetherby then the A58 to Leeds. After about 8 miles take the 3rd exit at the roundabout onto the A6120 Ring Road. Follow signs for Bradford for approximately 12 miles and at the 7th roundabout take the B6157 signposted Stanningley. Continue for ½ mile passing the Police Station on the left then turn left down New Street (at the Tradex Warehouse). Turn right into Newlands and the ground is situated at the end of the road next to a new housing development.

GATESHEAD FC

Founded: 1930 (Reformed in 1977)
Former Names: Gateshead United FC
Nickname: 'Tynesiders'
Ground: International Stadium, Neilson Road, Gateshead NE10 0EF
Record Attendance: 11,750 (vs Newcastle Utd, 1995)
Pitch Size: 110 × 70 yards

Colours: White shirts with Black shorts
Telephone N°: (0191) 477-1983
Ground Capacity: 11,750 (All seats)
Web site: www.gateshead-fc.com
E-mail: info@gateshead-fc.com

GENERAL INFORMATION

Car Parking: At the stadium
Coach Parking: At the stadium
Nearest Railway Station: Gateshead Stadium Metro (½ mile); Newcastle (British Rail) 1½ miles
Nearest Bus Station: Newcastle Coach Station, St. James' Boulevard, Newcastle-upon-Tyne, NE1 4BW (2½ miles)
Club Shop: At the stadium
Opening Times: Matchdays only
Telephone N°: (0191) 477-1983

GROUND INFORMATION

Away Supporters' Entrances & Sections: East Stand

ADMISSION INFO (2020/2021 PRICES)

Adult Seating: £15.00
Senior Citizen/Concessionary Seating: £8.00
Under-16s/Student Seating: £3.00
Under-12s: Admitted free of charge when accompanied by a paying adult

DISABLED INFORMATION

Wheelchairs: 5 spaces available each for home and away fans on the balcony (covered area)
Helpers: Admitted
Prices: Normal prices for the disabled. Helpers are admitted free of charge.
Disabled Toilets: Available in the Reception Area and on the 1st floor concourse – accessible by lift.
Contact: (0191) 477-1983 (Bookings are necessary)

Travelling Supporters' Information:
Routes: From the South: Take the A1(M) to Washington Services and fork right onto the A194(M) signposted Tyne Tunnel. At the next roundabout, turn left onto the A184 signposted for Gateshead. The Stadium is on the right after 3 miles.

GLOUCESTER CITY FC

Founded: 1883
Former Names: Gloucester YMCA
Nickname: 'The Tigers'
Ground: Meadow Park, Sudmeadow Road, Hempsted, Gloucester GL2 5HS
Record Attendance: 8,326 (1956)
Pitch Size: 112 × 72 yards

Colours: Yellow & Black Striped shirts with Black shorts
Telephone Nº: None
Ground Capacity: 3,648
Seating Capacity: 700
Web site: www.gloucestercityafc.com
E-mail: info@gcafc.co.uk

GENERAL INFORMATION
Car Parking: At the ground
Coach Parking: At the ground
Nearest Railway Station: Gloucester (1 mile)
Nearest Bus Station: Gloucester
Club Shop: At the ground
Opening Times: Matchdays only

GROUND INFORMATION
Away Supporters' Entrances & Sections:
No usual segregation

ADMISSION INFO (2020/2021 PRICES)
Adult Standing/Seating: £13.00
Under-18s Standing/Seating: £8.00
Under-16s Standing/Seating: £3.00
Under-11s: Admitted free of charge with a paying adult

DISABLED INFORMATION
Wheelchairs: Accommodated
Helpers: Admitted
Prices: Normal prices apply for disabled fans
Disabled Toilets: Available
Contact: info@gtafc.co.uk   (Bookings are necessary)

Travelling Supporters' Information:
Routes: Take the A40 into the City Centre towards the Historic Docks, then take Severn Road and turn right into Hempstead Lane. Take the second right into Sudmeadow Road and the ground is 50 yards on the left.

GUISELEY AFC

Founded: 1909
Former Names: None
Nickname: 'The Lions'
Ground: Nethermoor Park, Otley Road, Guiseley, Leeds LS20 8BT
Record Attendance: 3,366 (v Leeds United 26/7/18)
Pitch Size: 110 × 69 yards

Colours: White shirts with Royal Blue shorts and socks
Telephone Nº: 07507 750553 or (01943) 873223
Social Club Phone Nº: (01943) 872872
Ground Capacity: 4,000
Seating Capacity: 518
Web site: www.guiseleyafc.co.uk
E-mail: admin@guiseleyafc.co.uk

GENERAL INFORMATION

Car Parking: At the ground and in Netherfield Road – Please do not park in Ings Crescent!
Coach Parking: At the ground
Nearest Railway Station: Guiseley (5 minute walk)
Nearest Bus Station: Bus Stop outside the ground
Club Shop: At the ground
Opening Times: Matchdays only
Telephone Nº: (01943) 8773223

GROUND INFORMATION

Away Supporters' Entrances & Sections:
No usual segregation

ADMISSION INFO (2020/2021 PRICES)

Adult Standing/Seating: £13.00
Concessionary Standing/Seating: £9.00
Ages 11 to 18 Standing/Seating: £5.00
Under-11s Standing/Seating: £1.00 when accompanied by a paying adult
Programme Price: £3.00

DISABLED INFORMATION

Wheelchairs: 2 spaces are available in the Main Stand
Helpers: Admitted
Prices: Normal prices for disabled fans. Free for helpers
Disabled Toilets: None
Contact: Trudi Hannaford 07507 750583 (Bookings are advisable) – trudihannaford@guiseleyafc.co.uk

Travelling Supporters' Information:
Routes: Exit the M62 at Junction 28 and take the Leeds Ring Road to the roundabout at the junction of the A65 at Horsforth. Turn left onto the A65 and pass through Rawdon to Guiseley keeping Morrison's supermarket on your left. Pass straight through the traffic lights with the Station pub or your right and the ground is on the right after ¼ mile, adjacent to the cricket field.

HEREFORD FC

Founded: 1924	**Colours**: White shirts with Black shorts
Former Names: None	**Telephone Nº**: (01432) 268257
Nickname: 'United' 'The Bulls'	**Ground Capacity**: 5,213
Ground: Edgar Street, Hereford HR4 9JU	**Seating Capacity**: 3,390
Record Attendance: 18,114 (4th January 1958)	**Web site**: www.herefordfc.co.uk
Pitch Size: 110 × 70 yards	**E-mail**: info@herefordfc.co.uk

GENERAL INFORMATION

Car Parking: Merton Meadow Car Park (Near the ground)
Coach Parking: Merton Meadow Car Park
Nearest Railway Station: Hereford (½ mile)
Nearest Bus Station: Commercial Road, Hereford
Club Shop: At the ground
Opening Times: Wednesday and Friday 10.00am – 4.00pm.
Midweek home games, 10.00am–4.00pm & 6.00pm–7.30pm,
Saturday Matchdays 12.00pm to 2.45pm.
Telephone Nº: (01432) 268257

GROUND INFORMATION

Away Supporters' Entrances & Sections:
Edgar Street entrances for the Len Weston Stand and Terrace

ADMISSION INFO (2020/2021 PRICES)

Adult Standing: £14.00
Adult Seating: £16.00
Ages 16 to 18 Standing: £7.00
Ages 16 to 18 Seating: £8.00
Under-16s Standing/Seating: £2.00 (Under-5s free)
Concessionary Standing: £12.00
Concessionary Seating: £14.00

DISABLED INFORMATION

Wheelchairs: 7 spaces in total for Home and Away fans
Helpers: One helper admitted per disabled person
Prices: Concessionary prices for the disabled. Free for helpers
Disabled Toilets: Available in the Merton Stand
Contact: (01432) 268257 or 07596 263171 on Matchdays
E-mail: herefordfcdsa@gmail.com   (Bookings necessary)

Travelling Supporters' Information:
Routes: From the North: Follow A49 Hereford signs straight into Edgar Street; From the East: Take the A465 or A438 into
Hereford Town Centre, then follow signs for Leominster (A49) into Edgar Street; From the South: Take the A49 or A45 into the
Town Centre (then as East); From the West: Take the A438 into the Town Centre (then as East).

KETTERING TOWN FC

Founded: 1872
Former Names: Kettering FC
Nickname: 'The Poppies'
Ground: Latimer Park, Polwell Lane, Burton Latimer, Kettering NN15 5PS
Record Attendance: 11,526 (at Rockingham Road)
Pitch Size: 110 × 68 yards

Colours: Red and Black shirts with Black shorts
Telephone Nº: (01536) 217006
Ground Capacity: 2,500
Seating Capacity: 600
Web site: www.ketteringtownfc.com
E-mail: info@ketteringtownfc.com

GENERAL INFORMATION

Car Parking: At the ground
Coach Parking: At the ground
Nearest Railway Station: Kettering (3 miles)
Nearest Bus Station: Kettering
Club Shop: None

GROUND INFORMATION

Away Supporters' Entrances & Sections:
Station Road end when segregation is in force

ADMISSION INFO (2020/2021 PRICES)

Adult Standing/Seating: £15.00
Concessionary Standing/Seating: £10.00
Under-18s Standing/Seating: £2.00
Programme Price: £3.00

DISABLED INFORMATION

Wheelchairs: Accommodated around the ground
Helpers: Admitted
Prices: Normal prices apply for the disabled fans with registered carers admitted free of charge
Disabled Toilets: Available around the ground
Contact: 07881 827188 Neil Griffin (Secretary)
neil.griffin@ketteringtownfc.com

Travelling Supporters' Information:
Routes: The ground is located on the A6 about 350 yards north of the junction with the A45 (over the bridge). This is approximately 6 miles south of the A14.

KIDDERMINSTER HARRIERS FC

Founded: 1886
Nickname: 'Harriers'
Ground: Aggborough Stadium, Hoo Road, Kidderminster   DY10 1NB
Ground Capacity: 6,444
Seating Capacity: 3,140
Record Attendance: 9,155 (vs Hereford, 1948)

Pitch Size: 110 × 72 yards
Colours: Red shirts with White sleeves, Red shorts
Telephone Nº: (01562) 823931
Fax Number: (01562) 827329
Web Site: www.harriers.co.uk
E-mail: info@harriers.co.uk

GENERAL INFORMATION

Car Parking: At the ground (£3.00 to £5.00 per car)
Coach Parking: As directed
Nearest Railway Station: Kidderminster
Nearest Bus Station: Kidderminster Town Centre
Club Shop: At the ground
Opening Times: Weekdays 9.00am to 5.00pm. Saturday matchdays 11.00am to 3.00pm then 4.45pm to 5.30pm and midweek matchdays 9.00am to 8.00pm then for an hour after the game.
Telephone Nº: (01562) 823931

GROUND INFORMATION

Away Supporters' Entrances & Sections:
East Stand for seating and South Stand Terrace for standing

ADMISSION INFO (2020/2021 PRICES)

Adult Standing: £15.00
Adult Seating: £17.00
Concessionary Standing: £9.00
Concessionary Seating: £12.00
Under-16s Standing: £1.00
Under-16s Seating: £5.00
Programme: £3.00
Note: Under-5s are admitted free with a paying adult.

DISABLED INFORMATION

Wheelchairs: Home fans accommodated at the front of the Main Stand, Away fans in front of the East Stand
Helpers: Admitted
Prices: £10.00 for disabled fans. Helpers are admitted free
Disabled Toilets: Available by the disabled area
Contact: (01562) 823931   (Bookings are not necessary)

Travelling Supporters' Information:
Routes: Exit the M5 at Junction 3 and follow the A456 to Kidderminster. The ground is situated close by the Severn Valley Railway Station so follow the brown Steam Train signs and turn into Hoo Road about 200 yards downhill of the station. Follow the road along for ¼ mile and the ground is on the left.

LEAMINGTON FC

Founded: 1891
Former Names: Leamington Town FC,
Lockheed Borg & Beck FC, AP Leamington FC and
Lockheed Leamington FC
Nickname: 'The Brakes'
Ground: The Phillips 66 Community Stadium,
Harbury Lane, Leamington Spa CV33 9QB
Record Attendance: 2,102 (1st May 2017)

Colours: Gold and Black shirts with Black shorts
Telephone Nº: (01926) 430406
Ground Capacity: 2300
Seating Capacity: 294
Web Site: www.leamingtonfc.co.uk
E-mail: info@leamingtonfc.co.uk

GENERAL INFORMATION
Car Parking: At the ground
Coach Parking: At the ground
Nearest Railway Station: Leamington (4 miles)
Club Shop: At the ground plus online sales via the web site
Opening Times: Matchdays only

GROUND INFORMATION
Away Supporters' Entrances & Sections:
No usual segregation

ADMISSION INFO (2020/2021 PRICES)
Adult Standing/Seating: £13.00
Concessionary Standing/Seating: £9.00
Under-18s Standing/Seating: £3.00 (Under-12s free)
Student Standing/Seating: £6.00

DISABLED INFORMATION
Wheelchairs: 3 spaces available in the Main Stand
Helpers: Admitted
Prices: Normal prices apply for the disabled. Helpers are
admitted free of charge
Disabled Toilets: Available in the Clubhouse and Main Stand
Contact: (01926) 430406 (Bookings are not necessary)

Travelling Supporters' Information:
Routes: Exit the M40 at Junction 14 and take the A452 towards Leamington continuing at the roundabout into Europa Way (still A452). After approximately ½ mile, take the 4th exit at the roundabout into Harbury Lane (signposted for Harbury and Bishops Tachbrook). Continue on Harbury lane, taking the 3rd exit at the first roundabout and going straight ahead at the traffic lights. The ground is on the left hand side of the road after approximately 1½ miles.   **SatNav**: CV33 9SA

SOUTHPORT FC

Founded: 1881
Former Names: Southport Vulcan FC, Southport Central FC
Nickname: 'The Sandgrounders' and 'The Port'
Ground: The Pure Stadium, Haig Avenue, Southport, Merseyside   PR8 6JZ
Record Attendance: 20,010 (vs Newcastle, 1932)
Pitch Size: 110 × 77 yards

Colours: Yellow shirts with Black shorts
Telephone N°: (01704) 533422
Fax Number: (01704) 533455
Ground Capacity: 6,008
Seating Capacity: 1,660
Web site: www.southportfc.net
E-mail: james@southportfc.net

GENERAL INFORMATION

Car Parking: Street parking
Coach Parking: Adjacent to the ground
Nearest Railway Station: Meols Cop (½ mile)
Nearest Bus Station: Southport Town Centre
Club Shop: At the ground
Opening Times: Matchdays from 11.00am (from 6.30pm on evening matchdays)
Telephone N°: (01704) 533422

GROUND INFORMATION

Away Supporters' Entrances & Sections: Blowick End entrances

ADMISSION INFO (2020/2021 PRICES)

Adult Standing: £13.50
Adult Seating: £15.00
Concessionary Standing: £10.00
Concessionary Seating: £11.00
Under-19s Standing/Seating: £5.00
Note: Children aged 11 and under are admitted free of charge when accompanied by a paying adult.
Programme: £2.50

DISABLED INFORMATION

Wheelchairs: Accommodated in front of the Grandstand
Helpers: Admitted
Prices: Normal prices charged for the disabled. Helpers are admitted free of charge
Disabled Toilets: Available at the Blowick End of the Grandstand
Contact: (01704) 533422   (Bookings are not necessary)

Travelling Supporters' Information:
Routes: Exit the M58 at Junction 3 and take the A570 to Southport. At the major roundabout (McDonalds/Tesco) go straight on into Scarisbrick New Road, pass over the brook and turn right into Haig Avenue at the traffic lights. The ground is then on the right-hand side.

SPENNYMOOR TOWN FC

Founded: 2005 (Formed by the amalgamation of Evenwood Town and the defunct Spennymoor United)
Former Names: None
Nickname: 'The Moors'
Ground: The Brewery Field, Wood Vue, Spennymoor, Co. Durham   DL16 6JN
Record Attendance: 7,202 (30th March 1957)

Pitch Size: 104 × 65 yards
Colours: Black and White striped shirts, Black shorts
Telephone N°: (01388) 827248 or Club Secretary on 07421 472240
Ground Capacity: 3,000
Seating Capacity: 742
Web Site: www.spennymoortownfc.co.uk

GENERAL INFORMATION

Car Parking: Street parking sometimes available but fans are recommended to use the car parks behind the Town Hall and Leisure Centre or use the old Durham Road School for parking.
Coach Parking: Please contact Steven Lawson on 07871 206474 for information
Nearest Railway Station: Durham (6 miles)
Nearest Bus Station: Durham – the No. 6 bus which stops in Durham Road, Spennymoor (15 minute journey)
Club Shop: At the ground
Opening Times: Matchdays only
Telephone N°: (01388) 827248

GROUND INFORMATION

Away Supporters' Entrances & Sections:
Turnstile 7 for access to the Ramside Hall Estates Main Stand and the Motif8 Stand when segregation in is place.

ADMISSION INFO (2019/2020 PRICES)

Adult Standing/Seating: £10.00 – £14.00
Over-60s Standing/Seating: £8.00 – £9.00
Under-18s Standing/Seating: £3.00 – £4.00
Note: Prices vary depending on the category of the game. Under-10s are admitted free with a paying adult
Programme Price: £2.50

DISABLED INFORMATION

Wheelchairs: Accommodated by arrangement. Entrance via the Wood Vue turnstiles and Tees Crescent
Helpers: One helper admitted per wheelchair
Prices: Normal prices are charged for fans with disabilities. Helpers are admitted free of charge
Disabled Toilets: 2 available in the ground
Contact: 07871 206474 (Steven Lawson)

Travelling Supporters' Information:
Routes: Exit the A1(M) at Junction 60 and follow the A689 to Rushyford. Take the 3rd exit at the Rushyford roundabout onto the A167 then the 3rd exit at the Chilton roundabout, continuing on the A167 towards Spennymoor. Take the first exit at the Thinford roundabout onto the A688, carry straight on at the small roundabout then take the 3rd exit at the next roundabout into St. Andrew's Lane. Continue along St. Andrew's Lane, turning left at the first roundabout then take the 2nd exit at the mini-roundabout, passing Asda into King Street, and the 2nd exit at the next mini-roundabout into Durham Road. Bear right along Durham Road and Wood Vue is on the left after a short distance.

YORK CITY FC

Please note that the club are scheduled to move to the LNER Community Stadium during the early part of the 2020/21 season. However, as the new stadium is still undergoing testing, no fixed date for the move is known. The new stadium is located in Kathryn Avenue in the Huntington area of the city, post code: YO32 9AF Please contact the club for further information.

Founded: 1922
Nickname: 'The Minstermen'
Ground: Bootham Crescent, York   YO30 7AQ
Ground Capacity: 8,256   **Seating Capacity**: 3,409
Record Attendance: 28,123 (5th March 1938)
Pitch Size: 115 × 74 yards

Colours: Red shirts with Blue shorts
Telephone Nº: (01904) 624447 or (01904) 559500
Ticket Office: (01904) 559503 Extension 1
Fax Number: (01904) 631457
Web Site: www.yorkcityfootballclub.co.uk
E-mail: enquiries@yorkcityfootballclub.co.uk

GENERAL INFORMATION

Car Parking: Spaces are available in York Hospital car park (5 minutes walk) from 1.00pm (Saturday matches) and from 5.45pm (midweek matches). A voucher must be downloaded from the club's website to purchase a ticket and cost is £2.50.
Coach Parking: By Police direction
Nearest Railway Station: York (1 mile)
Club Shop: At the ground
Opening Times: Weekdays 11.00am – 3.00pm (but closed on Wednesdays); Saturday Matchdays 1.00pm–3.00pm and 4.40pm–5.30pm; Evening matches open from 6.00pm until kick-off then for 30 minutes after the final whistle.
Telephone Nº: (01904) 624447

GROUND INFORMATION

Away Supporters' Entrances & Sections:
Grosvenor Road turnstiles for Grosvenor Road End

ADMISSION INFO (2019/2020 PRICES)

Adult Standing: £14.00   **Adult Seating**: £15.00 – £19.00
Concessionary Standing: £10.00
Concessionary Seating: £11.00 – £14.00
Under-18s Standing: £5.00   **Seating**: £6.00 – £7.00
Under-5s Standing/Seating: Free of charge
Note: The above prices will also apply at the new stadium.

DISABLED INFORMATION

Wheelchairs: 18 spaces in total for Home & Away fans in the disabled section, in front of the Pitchside Bar. Use turnstile 13.
Helpers: One helper admitted per disabled person
Prices: Normal prices apply for disabled fans. Helpers free
Disabled Toilets: Available at entrance to the disabled area
Contact: (01904) 624447 (Ext. 1) (Bookings not necessary) or e-mail: slo@yorkcityfootballclub.co.uk

Travelling Supporters' Information:
Routes: From the North: Take the A1 then the A59 following signs for York. Cross the railway bridge and turn left after 2 miles into Water End. Turn right at the end following City Centre signs for nearly ½ mile then turn left into Bootham Crescent; From the South: Take the A64 and turn left after Buckles Inn onto the Outer Ring Road. Turn right onto the A19, follow City Centre signs for 1½ miles then turn left into Bootham Crescent; From the East: Take the Outer Ring Road turning left onto the A19. Then as from the South; From the West: Take the Outer Ring Road turning right onto the A19. Then as from the South.

THE VANARAMA NATIONAL LEAGUE SOUTH

Address

4th Floor, 20 Waterloo Street, Birmingham B2 5TB

Phone (0121) 643-3143

Web site www.footballconference.co.uk

Clubs for the 2020/2021 Season

BATH CITY FC

Founded: 1889
Former Names: Bath AFC, Bath Railway FC and Bath Amateurs FC
Nickname: 'The Romans'
Ground: Twerton Park, Bath   BA2 1DB
Record Attendance: 18,020 (1960 vs Brighton & HA)
Pitch Size: 110 × 76 yards

Colours: Black and White striped shirts, Black shorts
Telephone Nº: (01225) 423087
Ground Capacity: 3,528
Seating Capacity: 1,006
Web site: www.bathcityfc.com
E-mail: info@bathcityfootballclub.co.uk

GENERAL INFORMATION
Car Parking: 93 spaces available at the ground
Coach Parking: Available at the ground (Avon Street)
Nearest Railway Station: Oldfield Park (1 mile)
Nearest Bus Station: Dorchester Street, Bath
Club Shop: At the ground
Opening Times: Matchdays only
Telephone Nº: (01225) 423087

GROUND INFORMATION
Away Supporters' Entrances & Sections:
Turnstiles 17-19 for the Bristol End and Family Stand

ADMISSION INFO (2020/2021 PRICES)
Adult Standing: £14.00   **Adult Seating**: £15.00
Concessionary Standing: £11.00   **Seating**: £12.00
Student Standing: £8.00   **Student Seating**: £9.00
Under-16s Standing: £3.00   **Under-16s Seating**: £5.00

DISABLED INFORMATION
Wheelchairs: 10 spaces available each for home and away fans in front of the Family Stand
Helpers: Admitted
Prices: Concessionary prices are charged to disabled fans. Free for helpers
Disabled Toilets: 2 are available behind the Family Stand
Contact: (01225) 423087   (Bookings are necessary)

Travelling Supporters' Information:
Route: As a recommendation, avoid exiting the M4 at Junction 18 as the road takes you through Bath City Centre. Instead, exit the M4 at Junction 19 onto the M32. Turn off the M32 at Junction 1 and follow the A4174 Bristol Ring Road south then join the A4 for Bath. On the A4, after passing through Saltford you will reach a roundabout shortly before entering Bath. Take the 2nd exit at this roundabout then follow the road before turning left into Newton Road at the bottom of the steep hill. The ground is then on the right hand side of the road.

BILLERICAY TOWN FC

Founded: 1880
Former Names: None
Nickname: 'Town' 'Blues'
Ground: The Steel Team Stadium, New Lodge, Blunts Wall Road, Billericay, Essex CM12 9SA
Ground Capacity: 5,000   **Seating Capacity**: 2,000
Record Attendance: 4,582 (vs West Ham, 2017)

Colours: Shirts are Royal Blue with White trim, shorts are White with Royal Blue trim
Telephone N°: (01277) 286474
Web site: www.billericaytownfc.co.uk
E-mail: info@billericaytownfc.co.uk

GENERAL INFORMATION
Car Parking: Street parking only
Coach Parking: Please contact the club for information
Nearest Railway Station: Billericay (½ mile)
Club Shop: At the ground
Opening Times: Matchdays only
Telephone N°: (01277) 652188

GROUND INFORMATION
Away Supporters' Entrances & Sections:
No usual segregation

ADMISSION INFO (2020/2021 PRICES)
Adult Standing/Seating: £15.00
Senior Citizen & Student Standing/Seating: £10.00
Under-18s Standing/Seating: £5.00
Under-11s Standing/Seating: £1.00
Family Ticket: £25.00 (2 adults + 2 Under-11s)

DISABLED INFORMATION
Wheelchairs: Accommodated
Helpers: Admitted
Prices: Normal prices for disabled fans. Free for helpers
Disabled Toilets: Available in the Clubhouse and the ground
Contact: (01277) 286474   (Bookings are necessary)

Travelling Supporters' Information:
Route: Exit the M25 at Junction 28 and follow the A129 to Billericay. Turn right at the 1st set of traffic lights into Tye Common Road then 2nd right into Blunts Wall Road and the ground is on the right.
Alternative route: Exit the M25 at Junction 29 and take the A129 road from Basildon into Billericay and turn left at the 2nd set of traffic lights into Tye Common Road. Then as above.

BRAINTREE TOWN FC

Founded: 1898
Former Names: Manor Works FC, Crittall Athletic FC, Braintree & Crittall Athletic FC and Braintree FC
Nickname: 'The Iron'
Ground: Cressing Road Stadium, Clockhouse Way, Braintree, Essex   CM7 3DE
Record Attendance: 4,000 (May 1952)
Pitch Size: 110 × 70 yards

Ground Capacity: 4,222
Seating Capacity: 553
Colours: Orange shirts and socks with Blue shorts
Telephone N°: (01376) 345617
Web site: www.braintreetownfc.org.uk
E-mail: braintreetfc@aol.com

GENERAL INFORMATION
Car Parking: At the ground
Coach Parking: At the ground
Nearest Railway Station: Braintree (1 mile)
Nearest Bus Station: Braintree
Club Shop: At the ground
Opening Times: Matchdays only
Telephone N°: (01376) 345617

GROUND INFORMATION
Away Supporters' Entrances & Sections:
Gates 7-8 for accommodation in the Quag End

ADMISSION INFO (2020/2021 PRICES)
Adult Standing/Seating: £15.00
Concessionary Standing/Seating: £10.00
Under-18s Standing: £5.00

DISABLED INFORMATION
Wheelchairs: Accommodated – 6 spaces available in the Main Stand
Helpers: Admitted
Prices: Normal prices apply for fans with disabilities. Helpers are admitted free of charge
Disabled Toilets: Available
Contact: (01376) 345617

Travelling Supporters' Information:
Routes: Exit the A120 Braintree Bypass at the McDonald's roundabout and follow Cressing Road northwards. The floodlights at the ground are visible on the left ½ mile into town. Turn left into Clockhouse Way then left again for the ground.

CHELMSFORD CITY FC

Founded: 1938
Former Names: Chelmsford FC
Nickname: 'City' or 'Clarets'
Ground: Melbourne Community Stadium, Salerno Way, Chelmsford CM1 2EH
Record Attendance: 16,807 (at New Writtle Street)
Pitch Size: 109 × 70 yards

Colours: Claret and White shirts and shorts
Telephone Nº: (01245) 290959
Ground Capacity: 3,000
Seating Capacity: 1,400
Web site: www.chelmsfordcityfc.com
E-mail: enquiries@chelmsfordcityfc.com

GENERAL INFORMATION

Car Parking: Limited space at ground and street parking
Coach Parking: Two spaces available at the ground subject to advance notice
Nearest Railway Station: Chelmsford (2 miles)
Nearest Bus Station: Chelmsford (2 miles)
Club Shop: At the ground
Opening Times: Matchdays only
Telephone Nº: (01245) 290959

GROUND INFORMATION

Away Supporters' Entrances & Sections:
No usual segregation

ADMISSION INFO (2020/2021 PRICES)

Adult Standing/Seating: £15.00
Under-18s Standing/Seating: £5.00
Under-12s Standing/Seating: Free of charge
Concessionary Standing/Seating: £10.00
Note: Tickets are cheaper when purchased online

DISABLED INFORMATION

Wheelchairs: Spaces for 11 wheelchairs available
Helpers: Admitted free of charge
Prices: Normal prices apply for fans with disabilities
Disabled Toilets: Available
Contact: (01245) 290959 (Bookings are necessary)

Travelling Supporters' Information:
Route: The ground is situated next to the only set of high rise flats in Chelmsford which can therefore be used as a landmark. From the A12 from London: Exit the A12 at Junction 15 signposted for Chelmsford/Harlow/A414 and head towards Chelmsford along the dual-carriageway. At the third roundabout, immediately after passing the 'Superbowl' on the left, take the first exit into Westway, signposted for the Crematorium and Widford Industrial Estate. Continue along Westway which becomes Waterhouse Lane after the second set of traffic lights. At the next set of lights (at the gyratory system) take the first exit into Rainsford Road, signposted for Sawbridgeworth A1060. Continue along Rainsford Road then turn right into Chignal Road at the second set of traffic lights. Turn right again into Melbourne Avenue and Salerno Way is on the left at the end of the football pitches.

CHIPPENHAM TOWN FC

Founded: 1873
Former Names: None
Nickname: 'The Bluebirds'
Ground: Hardenhuish Park, Bristol Road, Chippenham, Wiltshire   SN14 6LR
Record Attendance: 4,800 (1951)
Pitch Size: 110 × 70 yards

Colours: Blue shirts, shorts and socks
Telephone Nº: (01249) 650400
Contact Nº: 07790 351004 (Club Secretary)
Ground Capacity: 3,000
Seating Capacity: 300
Web site: www.pitchero.com/clubs/chippenhamtown

GENERAL INFORMATION

Car Parking: Adjacent to the ground
Coach Parking: At the ground
Nearest Railway Station: Chippenham (1 mile)
Nearest Bus Station: Chippenham
Club Shop: At the ground
Opening Times: Matchdays only
Telephone Nº: (01249) 650400

GROUND INFORMATION

Away Supporters' Entrances & Sections:
No usual segregation

ADMISSION INFO (2020/2021 PRICES)

Adult Standing: £13.00
Adult Seating: £13.00
Concessionary/Student Standing: £9.00
Concessionary/Student Seating: £9.00
Under-18s Standing/Seating: £3.00
Note: Under-16s are admitted free of charge when accompanied by a paying adult.
Programme Price: £2.00

DISABLED INFORMATION

Wheelchairs: Accommodated at front of Stand
Helpers: Admitted
Prices: Normal prices apply for fans with disabilities. Helpers are admitted free of charge.
Disabled Toilets: Available in the Clubhouse
Contact: (01249) 650400   (Bookings are not necessary)

Travelling Supporters' Information:
Routes: Exit the M4 at Junction 17 and take the A350. Turn right at the first roundabout and follow the road to the junction with the A420. Turn left following 'Town Centre' signs and the ground is just over ½ mile on the left near the Pelican crossing.

CONCORD RANGERS FC

Founded: 1967
Former Names: None
Nickname: 'The Beachboys'
Ground: Aspect Arena, Thames Road, Canvey Island, SS8 0HH
Record Attendance: 1,537 (vs Mansfield Town, 2014)

Colours: Yellow shirts with Yellow shorts
Telephone Nº: (01268) 515750
Ground Capacity: 3,250
Seating Capacity: 375
Web Site: www.concordrangers.co.uk
E-mail: media@concordrangers.co.uk

GENERAL INFORMATION
Car Parking: At the ground
Coach Parking: At the ground
Nearest Railway Station: Benfleet
Club Shop: Online via the Club's web site only

GROUND INFORMATION
Away Supporters' Entrances & Sections:
No usual segregation

ADMISSION INFO (2020/2021 PRICES)
Adult Standing: £10.00
Adult Seating: £10.00
Concessionary Standing: £5.00
Concessionary Seating: £5.00
Note: Under-16s, NHS workers, Emergency workers and members of the Armed Forces are admitted free of charge.

DISABLED INFORMATION
Wheelchairs: Accommodated
Helpers: Admitted
Prices: Normal prices apply for the disabled and helpers
Disabled Toilets: Available
Contact: (01268) 515750   (Bookings are necessary)

Travelling Supporters' Information:
Routes: Take the A13 to the A130 (Canvey Way) for Canvey Island. At the Benfleet roundabout, take the 3rd exit into Canvey Road and continue along through Charfleets Service Road into Long Road. Take the 5th turn on the right into Thorney Bay Road and Thames Road is the 3rd turn on the right. The ground is on the left-hand side around 300 yards down Thames Road.

DARTFORD FC

Founded: 1888
Former Names: None
Nickname: 'The Darts'
Ground: Princes Park Stadium, Grassbanks, Darenth Road, Dartford DA1 1RT
Record Attendance: 4,097 (11th November 2006)
Pitch Size: 110 × 71 yards

Colours: White Shirts with Black Shorts
Telephone N°: (01322) 299991
Ground Capacity: 4,118
Seating Capacity: 640
Web Site: www.dartfordfc.com
E-mail: info@dartfordfc.com

GENERAL INFORMATION

Car Parking: At the ground
Coach Parking: At the ground
Nearest Railway Station: Dartford (½ mile)
Nearest Bus Station: Dartford (½ mile) & Bluewater (2 miles)
Club Shop: At the ground plus online sales
Opening Times: Matchdays only – 1.00pm to 6.00pm (but the stadium itself is open daily).
Telephone N°: (01322) 299991

ADMISSION INFO (2019/2020 PRICES)

Adult Standing: £14.00
Adult Seating: £14.00
Senior Citizen/Concessionary Standing: £9.00
Senior Citizen/Concessionary Seating: £9.00
Youth (Ages 13 to 17) Standing/Seating: £5.00
Junior (Ages 5 to 12) Standing/Seating: £2.00
Under-5s Standing/Seating: Free of charge

DISABLED INFORMATION

Wheelchairs: 9 spaces available in total around the ground
Helpers: Admitted
Prices: Normal prices for the disabled. Free for helpers
Disabled Toilets: Available behind each goal, in the main reception and on the upper floor.
Contact: (01322) 299991 (Bookings are not necessary)

Travelling Supporters' Information:
Routes: From M25 Clockwise: Exit the M25 at Junction 1B. At the roundabout, take the 3rd exit onto Princes Road (A225) then the second exit at the next roundabout.* Continue downhill to the traffic lights (with the ground on the left), turn left into Darenth Road then take the 2nd left for the Car Park; From M25 Anti-clockwise: Exit the M25 at Junction 2 and follow the A225 to the roundabout. Take the first exit at this roundabout then the 2nd exit at the next roundabout. Then as from * above.

DORKING WANDERERS FC

Photo courtesy of John Mills @ Altius Photography

Founded: 1999
Former Names: None
Nickname: 'Wanderers'
Ground: Meadowbank Stadium, Mill Lane, Dorking, RH4 1DX
Record Attendance: 1,604 (January 2020 vs Stockport County)
Pitch Size: 110 × 70 yards

Colours: Red and White striped shirts with Blue shorts
Telephone Nº: (01306) 400151
Ground Capacity: 3,000
Seating Capacity: 522
Web site: www.dorkingwanderers.com
E-mail: info@dorkingwanderers.com

GENERAL INFORMATION

Car Parking: Limited number of spaces at the ground. St. Martins Walk car park is 2 minutes walk from the stadium.
Coach Parking: Please contact the club for information.
Nearest Railway Station: Dorking West (½ mile)
Nearest Bus Station: Nearest bus stop is at The White Hart (Stop K)
Club Shop: At the ground
Opening Times: Matchdays only plus online sales
Telephone Nº: (01306) 400151

GROUND INFORMATION

Away Supporters' Entrances & Sections:
No usual segregation

ADMISSION INFO (2019/2020 PRICES)

Adult Standing/Seating: £12.00
Concessionary Standing/Seating: £9.00
Under-18s Standing/Seating: £4.00
Under-8s Standing/Seating: Free of charge
Programme Price: £2.00

DISABLED INFORMATION

Wheelchairs: Accommodated
Helpers: Admitted
Prices: Please contact the club for details
Disabled Toilets: Available
Contact: (01306) 400151   (Bookings are necessary)

Travelling Supporters' Information:
Routes: From the North: Exit the M25 at Junction 9 and follow the A24 southwards to Dorking. Upon reaching Dorking, take the 3rd exit at the Deepdene Roundabout onto the A25 (Reigate Road) and continue into the High Street. Turn right into Mill Lane by The White Horse pub for the ground; From the South: Follow the A24 northwards to Dorking. Take the first exit at the Deepdene Roundabout onto Reigate Road, then as above; From the West: Follow the A25 eastwards to Dorking, continue into the High Street, then turn right by The White Horse pub into Mill Lane for the ground; From the East: Follow the A25 westward into Dorking, continue into the High Street, then turn left into Mill Lane for the ground.

DULWICH HAMLET FC

Photo courtesy of John Mills @ Altius Photography

Founded: 1893
Former Names: None
Nickname: 'The Hamlet'
Ground: Champion Hill Stadium, Edgar Kail Way, London SE22 8BD
Record Attendance: 3,336 (8th November 2019 vs Carlisle United)
Pitch Size: 110 × 70 yards

Colours: Pink and Navy Blue quartered shirts with Navy Blue shorts
Telephone Nº: (0207) 274-8707
Ground Capacity: 3,000
Seating Capacity: 500
Web site: www.pitchero.com/clubs/dulwichhamlet

GENERAL INFORMATION

Car Parking: 50 spaces available at the ground
Coach Parking: At the ground
Nearest Railway Station: East Dulwich (adjacent)
Nearest Tube Station: Brixton (3½ miles)
Club Shop: At the ground
Opening Times: Matchdays only
Telephone Nº: (0207) 274-8707

GROUND INFORMATION

Away Supporters' Entrances & Sections:
No usual segregation

ADMISSION INFO (2019/2020 PRICES)

Adult Standing/Seating: £12.00
Concessionary Standing/Seating: £5.00
Note: Under-12s are admitted free of charge when accompanying a paying adult
Programme Price: £1.50

DISABLED INFORMATION

Wheelchairs: 10 spaces available in the front of the Main Stand
Helpers: Admitted
Prices: Normal prices apply for fans with disabilities. Helpers are admitted free of charge.
Disabled Toilets: Available behind the disabled area
Contact: (0207) 274-8707 (Bookings are necessary) – E-mail: commercial@dulwichhamletfc.co.uk

Travelling Supporters' Information:
Routes: From the Elephant & Castle: Go down Walworth Road, through Camberwell's one-way system and along Denmark Hill. Turn left by the railway into Champion Park and then right at the end down Grave Lane to the ground in Dog Kennel Hill; From the South: Come up through Streatham on the A23, turn right to Tulse Hill along the A205 (Christchurch Road) and carry on towards Sydenham. Turn left at The Grove into Lordship Lane and carry on to East Dulwich.

EASTBOURNE BOROUGH FC

Founded: 1963
Former Names: Langney Sports FC
Nickname: 'The Sports'
Ground: Langney Sports Club, Priory Lane, Langney, Eastbourne   BN23 7QH
Record Attendance: 3,770 (5th November 2005)
Pitch Size: 110 × 75 yards

Colours: Red and Black shirts with Red shorts
Telephone Nº: (01323) 766265
Ground Capacity: 4,151
Seating Capacity: 542
Web site: www.ebfc.co.uk
E-mail: info@ebfc.co.uk

GENERAL INFORMATION
Car Parking: Around 400 spaces available at the ground
Coach Parking: At the ground
Nearest Railway Station: Eastbourne (3 miles)
Nearest Bus Station: Eastbourne   (Service 6A to ground)
Club Shop: At the ground
Opening Times: Matchdays only
Telephone Nº: (01323) 766265

GROUND INFORMATION
Away Supporters' Entrances & Sections:
No usual segregation

ADMISSION INFO (2020/2021 PRICES)
Adult Standing: £13.00
Adult Seating: £13.00
Concessionary Standing/Seating: £9.00
Students/Under-18s Standing/Seating: £5.00
Under-13s Standing/Seating: £1.00

DISABLED INFORMATION
Wheelchairs: 6 spaces available
Helpers: Admitted
Prices: Normal prices apply for fans with disabilities. Free of charge for helpers
Disabled Toilets: Available
Contact: (01323) 766265   (Bookings are necessary)

Travelling Supporters' Information:
Routes: From the North: Exit the A22 onto the Polegate bypass, signposted A27 Eastbourne, Hastings & Bexhill. *Take the 2nd exit at the next roundabout for Stone Cross and Westham (A22) then the first exit at the following roundabout signposted Stone Cross and Westham. Turn right after ½ mile into Friday Street (B2104). At the end of Friday Street, turn left at the double mini-roundabout into Hide Hollow (B2191), passing Eastbourne Crematorium on your right. Turn right at the roundabout into Priory Road, and Priory Lane is about 200 yards down the road on the left; Approaching on the A27 from Brighton: Turn left at the Polegate traffic lights then take 2nd exit at the large roundabout to join the bypass. Then as from *.

EBBSFLEET UNITED FC

Founded: 1946
Former Names: Gravesend & Northfleet United FC, Gravesend United FC and Northfleet United FC
Nickname: 'The Fleet'
Ground: The Kuflink Stadium, Stonebridge Road, Northfleet, Gravesend, Kent   DA11 9GN
Record Attendance: 12,036 (vs Sunderland 1963)
Pitch Size: 112 × 72 yards

Colours: Reds shirts and shorts
Telephone Nº: (01474) 533796
Ground Capacity: 4,769
Seating Capacity: 2,179
Web site: www.ebbsfleetunited.co.uk
E-mail: info@eufc.co.uk

GENERAL INFORMATION

Car Parking: Ebbsfleet International Car Park C (when available) and also street parking
Coach Parking: At the ground
Nearest Railway Station: Northfleet (5 minutes walk)
Nearest Bus Station: Bus Stop outside the ground
Club Shop: At the ground plus online sales
Opening Times: Weekdays 9.00am to 5.00pm
Telephone Nº: (01474) 533796

GROUND INFORMATION

Away Supporters' Entrances & Sections:
Only certain games are segregated, when the Swanscombe End turnstiles are allocated to away supporters.
Please contact the club for further details

ADMISSION INFO (2020/2021 PRICES)

Adult Standing: £15.00
Adult Seating: £15.00
Concessionary Standing/Seating: £12.00
Under-17s Standing/Seating: £7.00
Under-12s Standing/Seating: £1.00 when accompanied by a paying adult (maximum of 2 per adult).

DISABLED INFORMATION

Wheelchairs: 6 spaces are available in the Disabled Area in front of the Main Stand
Helpers: Admitted free of charge
Prices: Normal prices apply for disabled fans
Disabled Toilets: Available in the Main Stand
Contact: (01474) 533796   (Bookings are necessary)

Travelling Supporters' Information:
Routes: Take the A2 to the Northfleet/Southfleet exit and follow signs for Northfleet (B262). Go straight on at the first roundabout then take the 2nd exit at the 2nd roundabout into Thames Way and follow the football signs for the ground.

HAMPTON & RICHMOND BOROUGH FC

Founded: 1921
Former Names: Hampton FC
Nickname: 'Beavers'
Ground: Jezzards Beveree Stadium, Beaver Close, off Station Road, Hampton, Middlesex TW12 2BX
Record Attendance: 3,225 (vs AFC Wimbledon, 2009)
Pitch Size: 113 × 71 yards

Colours: Blue and Red Striped shirts with Red shorts
Matchday Phone Nº: (020) 8979-2456
Ground Capacity: 3,500
Seating Capacity: 644
Web site: www.hamptonfc.net

GENERAL INFORMATION
Car Parking: At the ground and street parking
Coach Parking: Contact the Club for information
Nearest Railway Station: Hampton
Nearest Bus Station: Hounslow/Kingston/Fulwell
Club Shop: At the ground
Opening Times: Matchdays only
Telephone Nº: (020) 8979-2456

GROUND INFORMATION
Away Supporters' Entrances & Sections:
No usual segregation

ADMISSION INFO (2019/2020 PRICES)
Adult Standing: £13.00
Adult Seating: £13.00
Senior Citizen/Concessionary Standing: £8.00
Senior Citizen/Concessionary Seating: £8.00
Under-16s Standing/Seating: £3.00
Note: Under-5s are admitted free of charge
Programme Price: £2.50

DISABLED INFORMATION
Wheelchairs: Accommodated in front of the main stand
Helpers: Admitted
Prices: Normal prices apply
Disabled Toilets: Available
Contact: (020) 8979-2456 (Bookings are not necessary)

Travelling Supporters' Information:
Routes: From the South: Exit the M3 at Junction 1 and follow the A308 (signposted Kingston). Turn 1st left after Kempton Park into Percy Road. Turn right at the level crossing into Station Road then left into Beaver Close for the ground; From the North: Take the A305 from Twickenham then turn left onto the A311. Pass through Hampton Hill onto Hampton High Street. Turn right at the White Hart pub (just before the junction with the A308), then right into Station Road and right again into Beaver Close.

HAVANT & WATERLOOVILLE FC

Founded: 1998
Former Names: Formed by the amalgamation of Waterlooville FC and Havant Town FC
Nickname: 'The Hawks'
Ground: Westleigh Park, Martin Road, Havant, PO9 5TH
Record Attendance: 4,400 (2006/07)
Pitch Size: 111 × 70 yards

Colours: White shirts and shorts
Telephone Nº: (023) 9278-7822 (Ground)
Ground Capacity: 5,300
Seating Capacity: 710
Web site: www.havantandwaterloovillefc.co.uk
E-mail: generalmanager@havantandwaterloovillefc.co.uk

GENERAL INFORMATION
Car Parking: Space for 300 cars at the ground
Coach Parking: At the ground
Nearest Railway Station: Havant (1 mile)
Nearest Bus Station: Town Centre (1½ miles)
Club Shop: At the ground
Opening Times: Matchdays only
Telephone Nº: 07768 271143

GROUND INFORMATION
Away Supporters' Entrances & Sections:
No usual segregation

ADMISSION INFO (2020/2021 PRICES)
Adult Standing: £16.00
Adult Seating: £16.00
Concessionary Standing/Seating: £12.00
Under-20s Standing/Seating: £6.00
Note: When accompanied by a paying adult, children under the age of 12 are admitted free of charge

DISABLED INFORMATION
Wheelchairs: 12 spaces available in the Main Stand
Helpers: Admitted
Prices: Normal prices for disabled fans. Free for helpers
Disabled Toilets: Two available
Contact: (023) 9226-7822 (Bookings are necessary)

Travelling Supporters' Information:
Routes: From London or the North take the A27 from Chichester and exit at the B2149 turn-off for Havant. Take the 2nd exit off the dual carriageway into Bartons Road and then the 1st right into Martin Road for the ground; From the West: Take the M27 then the A27 to the Petersfield exit. Then as above.

HEMEL HEMPSTEAD TOWN FC

Founded: 1885
Former Names: Apsley FC and Hemel Hempstead FC
Nickname: 'The Tudors'
Ground: Vauxhall Road, Adeyfield, Hemel Hempstead HP2 4HW
Record Attendance: 2,840 (vs Gosport Borough 6th May 2013)
Pitch Size: 112 × 72 yards

Colours: Shirts and Shorts are Red with White trim
Telephone Nº: (01442) 251521 or (01442) 264300 (Greenacres Tavern)
Ground Capacity: 3,152
Seating Capacity: 534
Web site: www.hemelfc.com
E-mail: info@hemelfc.com

GENERAL INFORMATION

Car Parking: At the ground
Coach Parking: At the ground
Nearest Railway Station: Hemel Hempstead (1½ miles)
Nearest Bus Station: Hemel Hempstead (¾ mile)
Club Shop: At the ground
Opening Times: Matchdays only

GROUND INFORMATION

Away Supporters' Entrances & Sections:
No usual segregation

ADMISSION INFO (2020/2021 PRICES)

Adult Standing/Seating: £10.00
Concessionary Standing/Seating: £7.00
Under-18s Standing/Seating: £5.00 (£2.00 with an adult)
NHS Workers Standing/Seating: £5.00
Note: Under-12s are admitted for free with a paying adult
Programme Price: £2.50

DISABLED INFORMATION

Wheelchairs: Accommodated
Helpers: Admitted
Prices: Normal prices apply
Disabled Toilets: Available in the Clubhouse
Contact: 07858 990550   Dean Chance –
secretary@hemelfc.com

Travelling Supporters' Information:
Routes: Exit the M1 at Junction 8 and go straight ahead at the first roundabout. When approaching the 2nd roundabout move into the right hand lane and, as you continue straight across be ready to turn right almost immediately through a gap in the central reservation. This turn-off is Leverstock Green Road and continue along this to the double mini-roundabout. At this roundabout turn left into Vauxhall Road and the ground is on the right at the next roundabout.

HUNGERFORD TOWN FC

Founded: 1886
Former Names: Hungerford Swifts FC
Nickname: 'The Crusaders'
Ground: Town Ground, Bulpit Lane, Hungerford, RG17 0AY
Record Attendance: 1,684 (vs Sudbury Town)

Colours: White shirts with Black shorts
Contact Telephone Nº: (01488) 682939
Ground Capacity: 2,500
Seating Capacity: 170
Web: www.hungerfordtown.com
E-mail: smythjt@sky.com

GENERAL INFORMATION

Car Parking: At the ground and at the local school
Coach Parking: At the ground
Nearest Railway Station: Hungerford (½ mile)
Club Shop: At the ground
Opening Times: Matchdays only
Telephone Nº: (01488) 682939

GROUND INFORMATION

Away Supporters' Entrances & Sections:
No usual segregation

ADMISSION INFO (2020/2021 PRICES)

Adult Standing/Seating: £12.00
Concessionary Standing/Seating: £8.00
Under-18s Standing/Seating: £6.00
Under-16s Standing/Seating: £3.00
Note: Under-11s are admitted free of charge when accompanied by a paying adult
Programme Price: £2.00

DISABLED INFORMATION

Wheelchairs: Accommodated
Helpers: Admitted free of charge
Prices: Concessionary prices for the disabled.
Disabled Toilets: Available
Contact: (01488) 682939   (Bookings are not necessary) or 07585 770148 – John Smyth (General Secretary)

Travelling Supporters' Information:
Routes: Exit the M4 at Junction 14 and take the A338 towards Hungerford. Upon reaching Hungerford, turn right at the roundabout onto the A4 Bath Road, turn left at the next rounabout into Charnham Street then turn left again into Bridge Street (A338). The road becomes the High Street and pass under the railway line, carry straight on over three mini-roundabouts then take the next left into Priory Road. Continue to the end of the street and continue left into Priory Road then take the 3rd turning on the left into Bulpit Lane. The entrance to the ground is on the left shortly after crossing the junction with Priory Avenue.

MAIDSTONE UNITED FC

Founded: 1992 (Reformed)	**Colours**: Amber shirts with Black shorts
Former Names: Maidstone Invicta FC	**Telephone Nº**: (01622) 753817
Nickname: 'The Stones'	**Ground Capacity**: 4,191
Ground: Gallagher Stadium, James Whatman Way,	**Seating Capacity**: 750
Maidstone ME14 1LQ	**Web Site**: www.maidstoneunited.co.uk
Record Attendance: 4,101 (15th July 2017)	**E-mail**: itucker@maidstoneunited.co.uk

GENERAL INFORMATION

Car Parking: Various Pay & Display Car Parks available near the ground

Coach Parking: Maidstone coach park (1¼ miles) – please contact the club for further information

Nearest Railway Station: Maidstone East (¼ mile)

Club Shop: Available at the ground

Opening Times: Saturday Matchdays 12.30pm to 5.00pm; Tuesday Matchdays 6.15pm to 9.30pm.

Telephone Nº: (01622) 753817

GROUND INFORMATION

Away Supporters' Entrances & Sections:
No usual segregation – use the main turnstiles unless otherwise advertised. If segregation is in force, visiting fans should use turnstile 8 for accommodation in the North East Corner.

ADMISSION INFO (2020/2021 PRICES)

Adult Standing: £15.00

Adult Seating: £18.00

Senior Citizen/Student Standing: £12.00

Senior Citizen/Student Seating: £15.00

Ages 11 to 16 Standing: £7.00

Ages 11 to 16 Seating: £10.00

Under-11s Standing: £2.00

Under-11s Seating: £5.00

Programme Price: £2.00

DISABLED INFORMATION

Wheelchairs: Accommodated in the Manchett Main Stand and Genco Stand. The latter has 2 spaces for wheelchairs of away fans.

Helpers: Admitted

Prices: Normal prices apply for the disabled. Free for helpers

Disabled Toilets: Available

Contact: (01622) 753817   (Bookings are essential)

Travelling Supporters' Information:
Routes: Exit the M20 at Junction 6 or the M2 at Junction 3 and follow the A229 into Maidstone. After entering Maidstone, at the second roundabout (by the White Rabbit pub), take the third exit into James Whatman Way for the stadium. Please check the club web site for details of the nearest car parks.

OXFORD CITY FC

Founded: 1882
Former Names: None
Nickname: 'City'
Ground: Court Place Farm, Marsh Lane, Marston, Oxford   OX3 0NQ
Record Attendance: 9,500 (vs Leytonstone, 1950)

Colours: Blue & White hooped shirts with Blue shorts
Telephone Nº: (01865) 750906
Ground Capacity: 3,218
Seating Capacity: 520
Web Site: www.oxfordcityfc.co.uk
E-mail: club@oxcityfc.co.uk

GENERAL INFORMATION
Car Parking: At the ground
Coach Parking: At the ground
Nearest Railway Station: Oxford (3¾ miles)
Club Shop: At the ground
Opening Times: Matchdays only
Telephone Nº: (01865) 744493

GROUND INFORMATION
Away Supporters' Entrances & Sections:
No usual segregation

ADMISSION INFO (2020/2021 PRICES)
Adult Standing: £12.00
Adult Seating: £12.00
Concessionary/Student Standing: £6.00
Concessionary/Student Seating: £6.00
Under-16s Standing: £2.00
Under-16s Seating: £2.00
Note: Under-5s are admitted free of charge

DISABLED INFORMATION
Wheelchairs: Accommodated
Helpers: Admitted
Prices: Normal prices apply for the disabled and helpers
Disabled Toilets: Available
Contact: (01865) 744493   (Bookings are not necessary)

Travelling Supporters' Information:
Routes: The stadium is located by the side of the A40 Northern Bypass Road next to the Marston flyover junction to the north east of Oxford. Exit the A40 at the Marston junction and head into Marsh Lane (B4150). Take the first turn on the left into the OXSRAD Complex then turn immediately left again to follow the approach road to the stadium in the far corner of the site.

SLOUGH TOWN FC

Image courtesy of Gary House Photography

Founded: 1890
Former Names: Slough FC and Slough United FC
Nickname: 'The Rebels'
Ground: Arbour Park, Stoke Road, Slough SL2 5AY
Record Attendance: 1,950
(vs Rochdale, 4/12/2017)
Contact Telephone Nº: 07792 126124

Colours: Shirts are Amber with Navy Blue sleeves, shorts are Navy Blue
Ground Capacity: 2,000
Seating Capacity: 548
Web site: www.sloughtownfc.net
E-mail: gensec@sloughtownfc.net

GENERAL INFORMATION

Car Parking: At the ground, at St. Joseph's Catholic High School and in other local car parks
Coach Parking: At the ground
Nearest Railway Station: Slough (¾ mile)
Nearest Bus Station: Slough (¾ mile)
Club Shop: At the ground
Opening Times: Matchdays only
Telephone Nº: 07933 221337 (Sue Shiel)

GROUND INFORMATION

Away Supporters' Entrances & Sections:
No usual segregation

ADMISSION INFO (2020/2021 PRICES)

Adult Standing/Seating: £13.00
Concessions Standing/Seating: £9.00
Under-18s Standing/Seating: £5.00
Under-16s Standing/Seating: £3.00 (Under-5s free)
Note: Under-12s must be accompanied by an adult.
Programme Price: £1.50

DISABLED INFORMATION

Wheelchairs: Accommodated (enter via the front entrance)
Helpers: Admitted. A free carers pass is available.
Download the relevant form from the club's web site.
Prices: Normal prices apply for the disabled and helpers
Disabled Toilets: Available
Contact: 07792 126124 (Bookings are not necessary) –
E-mail: gensec@sloughtownfc.net

Travelling Supporters' Information:
Routes: From the South: Exit the M4 at Junction 5 and head west on the A4 (London Road) for approximately 2¾ miles. Pass the Tesco Extra store and the turning to Slough Railway station on your right then turn right onto Stoke Road (B416). Continue along Stoke Road for ¾ mile then Arbour Park is on the right; From the North: Exit the M40 at Junction 2 and head south on the A355 towards Slough. After approximately 1½ miles, turn left onto Parish Lane by the Indian Courtyard and at the end of the road, turn right onto Windsor Road (B416). After 2 miles take the second exit at the roundabout, continuing on the B416 and Arbour Park is on the left after approximately 1 mile.

ST. ALBANS CITY FC

Founded: 1908
Former Names: None
Nickname: 'The Saints'
Ground: Clarence Park, York Road, St. Albans, Hertfordshire AL1 4PL
Record Attendance: 9,757 (27th February 1926)
Pitch Size: 110 × 80 yards

Colours: Yellow shirts with Blue trim, Blue shorts
Telephone N°: (01727) 848914
Fax Number: (01727) 848914
Ground Capacity: 5,007
Seating Capacity: 667
Web site: www.stalbanscityfc.com
E-mail: Contact the club via the form on the website

GENERAL INFORMATION

Car Parking: Street parking or in the railway station car park (£2.50 charge)
Coach Parking: In Clarence Park
Nearest Railway Station: St. Albans City (200 yds)
Club Shop: At the ground
Opening Times: Matchdays only
Telephone N°: (01727) 848914

GROUND INFORMATION

Away Supporters' Entrances & Sections:
No usual segregation but the South Stand can be used for away fans if necessary.

ADMISSION INFO (2020/2021 PRICES)

Adult Standing/Seating: £16.50
Concessionary Standing/Seating: £11.00
Under-16s Standing/Seating: £6.00
Note: Under-12s are admitted free of charge when accompanied by a paying adult
Programme Price: £2.50

DISABLED INFORMATION

Wheelchairs: Accommodated
Helpers: One admitted per disabled supporter
Prices: Normal prices for the disabled. Helpers free of charge
Disabled Toilets: Available in the York Road End
Contact: (01727) 848914   (Bookings are not necessary)

Travelling Supporters' Information:
Routes: Take the M1 or M10 to the A405 North Orbital Road and at the roundabout at the start of the M10, go north on the A5183 (Watling Street). Turn right along St. Stephen's Hill and carry along into St. Albans. Continue up Holywell Hill, go through two sets of traffic lights and at the end of St. Peter's Street, take a right turn at the roundabout into Hatfield Road. Follow over the mini-roundabouts and at the second set of traffic lights turn left into Clarence Road and the ground is on the left. Park in Clarence Road and enter the ground via the Park or in York Road and use the entrance by the footbridge.

TONBRIDGE ANGELS FC

Founded: 1948
Former Names: Tonbridge FC
Nickname: 'The Angels'
Ground: The Halcyon Wealth Consmead Stadium, Darenth Avenue, Tonbridge   TN10 3JF
Record Attendance: 2,411 (7th May 2011)

Colours: Blue and White shirts with White shorts
Telephone N°: (01732) 352417
Ground Capacity: 3,014
Seating Capacity: 774
Web site: www.tonbridgeangels.co.uk
E-mail: charlie.cole@tonbridgeangels.co.uk

GENERAL INFORMATION
Car Parking: At the ground
Coach Parking: At the ground
Nearest Railway Station: Tonbridge (2 miles)
Club Shop: At the ground
Opening Times: Matchdays only plus online sales
Telephone N°: (01732) 352417

GROUND INFORMATION
Away Supporters' Entrances & Sections:
No usual segregation

ADMISSION INFO (2019/2020 PRICES)
Adult Standing: £13.00
Adult Seating: £14.00
Student/Senior Citizen Standing: £9.00
Student/Senior Citizen Seating: £10.00
Under-12s Standing: £4.00
Under-12s Seating: £5.00

DISABLED INFORMATION
Wheelchairs: Accommodated
Helpers: Admitted
Prices: Normal prices apply
Disabled Toilets: One available
Contact: (01732) 352417

Travelling Supporters' Information:
Routes: Take the A26 or A21 to Tonbridge Town Centre, pass through the High Street and head north up Shipbourne Road which is the A227 Gravesend road. Turn left at the 2nd mini-roundabout by the 'Pinnacles' Pub into Darenth Avenue. The ground is situated at the bottom end of Darenth Avenue.

WELLING UNITED FC

Founded: 1963
Former Names: None
Nickname: 'The Wings'
Ground: Park View Road, Welling, Kent DA16 1SY
Record Attendance: 4,100 (vs Gillingham, 1989)
Pitch Size: 112 × 72 yards

Colours: Shirts are Red with White trim, Red shorts
Telephone Nº: (0208) 301-1196
Ground Capacity: 4,500
Seating Capacity: 1,000
Web site: www.wellingunited.com

GENERAL INFORMATION

Car Parking: Street parking only
Coach Parking: Outside of the ground
Nearest Railway Station: Welling (¾ mile)
Nearest Bus Station: Bexleyheath
Club Shop: At the ground
Opening Times: Matchdays only
Telephone Nº: (0208) 301-1196

GROUND INFORMATION

Away Supporters' Entrances & Sections:
Accommodation in the Danson Park End and the East Stand

ADMISSION INFO (2019/2020 PRICES)

Adult Standing: £13.00   **Adult Seating**: £15.00
Concessionary Standing: £9.00
Concessionary Seating: £11.00
Under-18s Standing: £5.00
Under-18s Seating: £7.00
Under-12s Standing: Free with a paying adult
Under-12s Seating: £2.00 with a paying adult
Programme Price: £3.00

DISABLED INFORMATION

Wheelchairs: Accommodated at the side of the Main Stand
Helpers: Admitted
Prices: Concessionary prices for fans with disabilities.
Helpers are admitted free of charge
Disabled Toilets: Yes
Contact: (0208) 301-1196   (Bookings are not necessary)

Travelling Supporters' Information:
Routes: Take the A2 (Rochester Way) from London, then the A221 Northwards (Danson Road) to Bexleyheath. At the end turn left towards Welling along Park View Road and the ground is on the left.

National League — 2019/2020 Season

	AFC Fylde	Aldershot Town	Barnet	Barrow	Boreham Wood	Bromley	Chesterfield	Chorley	Dagenham & Redbridge	Dover Athletic	Eastleigh	Ebbsfleet United	Halifax Town	Harrogate Town	Hartlepool United	Maidenhead United	Notts County	Solihull Moors	Stockport County	Sutton United	Torquay United	Woking	Wrexham	Yeovil Town
AFC Fylde	■	1-0	0-4	0-1	1-2		1-3	0-0	3-0	0-0	3-1	1-0		0-0			1-2	0-0	1-2	0-0	2-3	1-4	3-2	
Aldershot Town	1-2	■	0-0	1-2	3-2	0-1	2-2	3-3	0-1	4-0	3-1		1-1	1-1	0-3	2-0	2-1		2-1	1-1			1-0	1-3
Barnet	2-1	2-0	■		2-2	1-2	2-2	2-1		0-1		5-2	1-1		2-1	1-0		0-0	1-2		2-2	2-2		1-0
Barrow	1-1	1-0	2-1	■	3-1	2-0		2-2	2-1	1-0	2-0	7-0	1-2	0-3	0-1	2-0	0-2	3-0		1-0	2-1			1-0
Boreham Wood	0-2	0-0	0-0	1-1	■		2-2		3-1	2-2	1-2		2-1	1-1	2-1	1-2	1-0	4-0	0-1		1-0	2-2		1-0
Bromley	2-2		1-2	1-2	1-0	■	2-1		3-0	3-0	2-3	3-1	5-0	3-3			2-1	2-2	2-2	0-1	3-3	1-0	0-2	1-1
Chesterfield	1-1	2-1		2-2		1-2	■	2-3	1-1	1-2	1-2	4-0	2-3	3-4	1-5		1-0	2-2		1-0	1-0	1-2	3-2	1-2
Chorley		0-0	0-1	1-3	1-3	0-0	1-2	■	1-0	1-1	0-2	0-4	0-1	0-2	0-0		1-6	3-0		1-0	1-1	0-2	1-2	
Dagenham & Redbridge	1-2	6-1	1-1	0-2	0-3	1-1		0-0	■		1-1		4-2	3-1	1-2	2-0	2-0	1-1	1-2	0-0	0-2	2-1		3-2
Dover Athletic	5-1	2-0		2-1	0-2	3-0	1-1	1-1	1-2	■	3-1	1-1	0-2		1-1	3-4	2-2	1-1	0-1		1-2	1-2	2-1	0-1
Eastleigh	2-2	0-0	1-2		2-0	1-1	0-2	0-0	1-1		■	1-1		4-2	1-1	2-1	1-0			1-1	3-2	2-0		0-2
Ebbsfleet United		1-2	3-0	0-3		2-2	1-0	5-5	0-1	1-1	1-1	■	1-4	0-2	2-2	1-2	2-2		0-1	1-1	2-4	2-1	2-1	1-3
Halifax Town	4-1		4-2	0-2		2-1	1-0	0-0	1-0	4-2	1-1	0-1	■	0-1	2-0	5-2	2-4	0-0	1-0	2-4	0-2			0-2
Harrogate Town		1-0	2-1		0-0	1-1	3-1	2-0		0-2	3-0	2-0	2-2	■	4-1	1-0	0-2	2-2	2-1	2-0	2-1		0-2	3-0
Hartlepool United	2-2	2-0	2-0	2-2		2-3	3-1		1-0	0-2	2-1	0-1		0-1	■	2-0		2-0	1-3		1-1	4-2		2-1
Maidenhead United	1-1	1-2	1-4	0-4	0-1	1-2		4-1	1-2		1-3	0-1	1-1	0-1	1-1	■	0-0	1-0	1-2			2-3	2-0	
Notts County	2-0	3-1	1-2	0-3	2-2	2-1	3-0	5-1	2-0	0-0	4-0		1-0		2-2	3-0	■	0-0	1-1	1-1	2-0	1-1	1-1	
Solihull Moors	3-1	2-1	1-0	0-0	0-2	2-1	3-0		2-1	3-0	1-2	2-1		0-1	0-2	0-1		■	2-0	2-0	3-0		3-1	0-1
Stockport County	2-1	1-2	1-1	3-2	1-3	1-0	2-0	4-2	1-0	0-2	2-0	1-1	5-1		2-1	0-1	1-4		■	0-0	0-4	1-3		
Sutton United		1-1	2-2		0-2	4-0	2-2	0-2	1-2			2-3	0-1	3-1	1-1	0-3	1-1	0-0	0-0	■	2-0	6-2	3-1	3-2
Torquay United	2-1	2-0		4-2	2-1		0-3	2-0	0-0		2-3	0-0	1-0	4-2	1-2	0-2			1-5	1-2	■	4-1	1-0	0-2
Woking		0-1	1-3	3-2	1-2	2-1		1-0			1-1	2-2	0-0	1-0	2-1	2-0	0-4	2-0	1-1	0-2	1-1	■	1-1	1-0
Wrexham	0-1	1-2	1-1	2-1		1-0	0-1	3-1	0-0		0-0	1-0	1-0	1-1		2-2		2-0	1-2	1-1		3-0	■	3-3
Yeovil Town	3-2	2-2			1-1	3-1		1-1	0-1	1-0		2-0	1-2	2-2	1-2	3-1	0-0	1-1	1-0	6-2	3-1	3-0		■

National League
Season 2019/2020

Barrow	37	21	7	9	68	39	70	1.89
Harrogate Town	37	19	9	9	61	44	66	1.78
Notts County	38	17	12	9	61	38	63	1.66
Yeovil Town	37	17	9	11	61	44	60	1.62
Boreham Wood	37	16	12	9	55	40	60	1.62
Halifax Town	37	17	7	13	50	49	58	1.57
Barnet	35	14	12	9	52	42	54	1.54
Stockport County	39	16	10	13	51	54	58	1.49
Solihull Moors	38	15	10	13	48	37	55	1.45
Woking	38	15	10	13	50	55	55	1.45
Dover Athletic	38	15	9	14	49	49	54	1.42
Hartlepool United	39	14	13	12	56	50	55	1.41
Bromley	38	14	10	14	57	52	52	1.37
Torquay United	36	14	6	16	56	61	48	1.33
Sutton United	38	12	14	12	47	42	50	1.32
Eastleigh	37	11	13	13	43	55	46	1.24
Dagenham & Redbridge	37	11	11	15	40	44	44	1.19
Aldershot Town	39	12	10	17	43	55	46	1.18
Wrexham	37	11	10	16	46	49	43	1.16
Chesterfield	38	11	11	16	55	65	44	1.16
Maidenhead United	38	12	5	21	44	58	41	1.08
Ebbsfleet United	39	10	12	17	47	68	42	1.08
AFC Fylde	37	9	12	16	44	60	39	1.05
Chorley	38	4	14	20	31	65	26	0.68

Play was suspended on 16th March 2020 due to the Covid-19 pandemic and then ended early on 20th April 2020. Final league positions were therefore decided on a Points won Per Game basis.

National League Promotion Play-offs

Boreham Wood	2	Halifax Town	1
Yeovil Town	0	Barnet	2

Harrogate Town	1	Boreham Wood	0
Notts County	2	Barnet	0

Harrogate Town	3	Notts County	1

Promoted: Barrow and Harrogate Town

Relegated: Ebbsfleet United, AFC Fylde and Chorley

National League North 2019/2020 Season

	AFC Telford United	Alfreton Town	Altrincham	Blyth Spartans	Boston United	Brackley Town	Bradford Park Avenue	Chester	Curzon Ashton	Darlington	Farsley Celtic	Gateshead	Gloucester City	Guiseley	Hereford	Kettering Town	Kidderminster Harriers	King's Lynn Town	Leamington	Southport	Spennymoor Town	York City
AFC Telford United	■	3-0	2-2	4-2	1-3	0-1		1-3		1-2	0-2	0-0	4-3	4-1		3-1	2-0	1-3	1-3		2-2	1-1
Alfreton Town	1-1	■	3-0	1-1	2-4	4-0		3-2	1-2	2-4		6-1		2-0	0-2			2-2	1-0	2-0	0-2	1-3
Altrincham	5-2	3-2	■	3-1		2-0		2-1	1-1	3-1	3-0		1-1	5-1	1-1	1-1			5-0	3-0	4-1	1-3
Blyth Spartans	3-1		0-3	■	0-1	0-6		2-2	2-1	0-2	2-0	3-3	1-2	1-4	0-1			1-1	0-3		1-4	0-3
Boston United	1-0		5-0	2-0	■	1-0	2-1	1-1	0-0		0-3		1-1		2-1	2-0	0-3	1-0	2-0			3-1
Brackley Town	1-1	1-0	1-0	5-2	0-0	■	8-0	1-1	3-0	5-1	0-1		3-0	0-0		1-1	2-0	1-1		1-1	0-0	
Bradford (Park Avenue)	2-3		2-0	0-0	1-2	1-2	■	2-1	0-2		0-3		1-2	0-5	3-2		0-3	2-3	0-3	0-3	1-1	0-2
Chester	0-0	3-0	1-1	2-1		2-3	2-1	■	0-1	3-0	2-1		4-0	3-1	4-1			3-2	3-3	4-0		0-1
Curzon Ashton	2-1	0-2	0-1	0-1	1-1	0-4	5-0	1-3	■	3-1	4-0	0-1			2-0	0-0	0-1				1-1	1-0
Darlington	2-3	3-0		2-1	2-1	1-1	0-1	2-0		■	2-4	1-2	1-2	0-0	3-0	1-0			2-0	2-1	0-2	
Farsley Celtic	1-1	1-1		2-0	2-4	1-1	5-0		2-1	3-1	■		1-1	0-1	1-2	3-2	0-1	1-2	2-1	0-3	1-0	
Gateshead		3-1	2-0	2-3	3-0	2-0	1-1	2-0	3-0		0-3	■		1-0	2-3	2-0		0-0	1-2	4-2	0-0	1-0
Gloucester City	0-1		1-1		3-0		1-0		2-2	2-1			■	3-1	0-2	2-2			2-1	0-1	1-2	2-3
Guiseley	1-2	2-4	1-1		0-2		0-1	1-0	1-2	2-0	2-2	2-1		■	3-0	1-2	1-2	3-0	3-0		3-1	0-0
Hereford	1-0	1-2	0-2		0-0	1-1	1-1		1-1	2-2	1-1	2-1		0-0	■	1-0	2-1		1-2	2-2	2-2	2-2
Kettering Town	2-1	2-1	0-2	4-4	0-2		4-0	1-1	0-0		1-0	1-2	1-1		0-0	■	3-5				0-2	0-0
Kidderminster Harriers		0-1	2-0	0-1	1-3	1-3		0-1		1-1	2-0	1-2	2-3		3-1		■	2-4	2-2	0-1	1-1	0-1
King's Lynn Town		3-2	2-2	3-0	1-0			0-1	2-2	4-1	2-0	1-0	2-2	0-1	3-1	2-1	0-2	■	5-2		3-0	1-0
Leamington		0-1	0-1	2-0		2-0		0-0	1-1	3-0	0-3	0-0	3-0	2-2	0-2	3-1		0-0	■		1-0	2-2
Southport	0-1		2-1	2-0	1-3	1-0	3-3	1-3	0-0			1-0	3-0	3-2	1-1	1-2	1-2	4-1		■		0-2
Spennymoor Town	3-3	5-0	3-2	5-0	2-1	0-0	3-0	2-1		3-1		1-3	5-1		4-0	1-2	2-1	2-2	2-0	1-0	■	1-4
York City	2-0	1-0			2-1	1-0	2-1	4-2	1-1	0-1	0-0	1-1		1-2	1-4	1-0	1-1	3-0	2-0	1-1		■

National League North

Season 2019/2020

	P	W	D	L	F	A	Pts	PPG
King's Lynn Town	32	19	7	6	63	39	64	2.00
York City	34	19	9	6	52	28	66	1.94
Boston United	32	17	7	8	46	32	58	1.81
Brackley Town	34	16	12	6	61	25	60	1.76
Altrincham	33	16	9	8	62	40	57	1.73
Chester	32	15	9	8	58	38	54	1.69
Gateshead	31	14	10	7	47	31	52	1.68
Spennymoor Town	34	15	10	9	63	45	55	1.62
Guiseley	33	14	8	11	52	41	50	1.52
Darlington	33	14	6	13	43	50	48	1.45
Farsley Celtic	34	14	6	14	50	45	48	1.41
Southport	32	12	7	13	40	41	43	1.34
Alfreton Town	32	12	4	16	48	55	40	1.25
AFC Telford United	34	11	9	14	51	56	42	1.24
Kidderminster Harriers	33	10	8	15	39	43	38	1.15
Hereford	35	9	12	14	39	56	39	1.11
Gloucester City	30	9	6	15	39	57	33	1.10
Leamington	32	9	8	15	39	51	35	1.09
Kettering Town	31	7	11	13	36	46	32	1.03
Curzon Ashton	33	8	10	15	34	42	34	1.03
Blyth Spartans	33	6	5	22	32	78	23	0.70
Bradford Park Avenue	33	5	5	23	25	80	20	0.61

Play was suspended on 16th March 2020 due to the Covid-19 pandemic and the season ended early on 20th April 2020. Final league positions were therefore decided on a Points won Per Game basis.

National League North Promotion Play-offs

Altrincham 3   Chester 2
Brackley Town 1   Gateshead 1
Gateshead won 7-6 on penalties.

York City 0   Altrincham 2
Boston United 5   Gateshead 3

Boston United 0   Altrincham 1

Promoted: King's Lynn Town and Altrincham

There was no relegation out of the National League this season

75

National League South 2019/2020 Season	Bath City	Billericay Town	Braintree Town	Chelmsford City	Chippenham Town	Concord Rangers	Dartford	Dorking Wanderers	Dulwich Hamlet	Eastbourne Borough	Hampton & Richmond Boro	Havant & Waterlooville	Hemel Hempstead Town	Hungerford Town	Maidstone United	Oxford City	Slough Town	St. Albans City	Tonbridge Angels	Wealdstone	Welling United	Weymouth
Bath City	■	2-1	2-0		3-2	3-1	3-0	1-0	3-2	2-2	3-0		2-0	2-1	1-1	1-2		0-3	0-0	0-0		0-0
Billericay Town	1-1	■	2-1	1-1			2-2		1-0		0-1		3-0		1-1	2-2	3-2	3-3	3-1	2-1	1-1	1-1
Braintree Town	2-0	2-3	■	1-2		0-1	3-2	2-1	5-0	0-4	3-3	0-0	0-3	1-1	1-0	0-1	0-1	0-1		0-4		1-1
Chelmsford City	1-0	1-1	4-1	■	3-3	1-1	4-0	2-2	1-1	1-1	4-1		2-1	4-1		2-6	1-1			1-3	1-1	
Chippenham Town	1-3	2-0	1-2	2-1	■	3-0	1-5	0-2	2-2			0-0	2-2		1-0	1-1	0-3	2-1	2-1	1-1	0-0	1-0
Concord Rangers	0-1	4-1	2-2	2-1	0-1	■		0-2	3-3		5-0	0-2	0-0	3-1	0-2	0-1		2-1		3-3		3-0
Dartford		3-2	2-1	3-0	1-1	0-1	■	3-4	1-0	2-1	1-2	1-1	1-1		2-2	3-0	2-3	1-1	3-0	0-0		4-0
Dorking Wanderers	0-0		4-4	2-0	1-0		2-3	■	0-0	4-0	0-1	1-2	3-1	1-0	3-1	0-2	3-5		3-1	2-2	2-0	1-0
Dulwich Hamlet	1-3	0-1	6-0	5-3	1-1	2-2	1-1		■	1-2	1-3	2-1	2-3	0-1		2-3	2-1	0-1		1-0	0-1	2-2
Eastbourne Borough	1-2	1-1		0-4	2-1	2-2	0-2	3-2	0-3	■	4-1		1-1		3-0	1-1	0-2	3-3	2-0		2-1	1-1
Hampton & Richmond Boro	0-0	1-1			1-0	2-3	1-2		0-3		■	3-4	1-2	7-1	2-1	1-1	1-2	2-1	1-0	2-0	1-1	2-3
Havant & Waterlooville	2-1		1-3	0-0	2-1	2-1		6-0	0-0	0-0	2-0	■	1-2	3-1	1-2		1-0	1-2		2-4	1-1	
Hemel Hempstead Town	2-1	3-0	0-3	2-0	0-1	1-0		1-0	1-0	1-1		1-2	■	4-1			1-1	1-0	1-1	0-3	0-2	0-1
Hungerford Town	0-1		2-0	1-0	1-1		2-2	0-1	1-4	0-1	0-2	1-3		■	1-3	1-2	1-0	1-2	1-0		1-2	
Maidstone United	0-2	2-1	1-0	4-1	0-0			2-3	4-1	0-0	1-2	2-2	1-1		■	1-0	1-1	4-0	2-2		3-1	1-2
Oxford City		2-2	1-4		1-3	0-3	0-1	2-1	2-1		3-2	0-3	1-2	3-2	1-4	■	2-1	3-3	0-3	3-2		0-0
Slough Town	3-2	3-1	1-0	2-1			1-0	0-1		1-1	3-1	1-1	2-0	0-2		0-1	■	1-1	0-0	2-1	1-0	1-1
St. Albans City	0-1		0-3	1-1	0-0	2-1	1-2	1-1		1-3	1-1	1-3	2-0	2-2	1-0	0-0		■	2-3	1-2		1-4
Tonbridge Angels		3-2	5-1	1-2	3-2	1-0	3-2		1-2				1-3	0-2	1-1		4-4		■	2-1		1-1
Wealdstone	7-0	3-0		0-1	1-0	3-0	4-1	3-1	2-1	2-0		1-4		3-1	2-1	1-0	2-1	1-0	3-1	■	1-0	
Welling United	0-3	2-0	6-2		1-0		0-3	2-1	0-0	0-0	0-1		2-0	3-2	1-0	3-1	1-2	0-1	4-2	1-2	■	1-3
Weymouth	1-1	0-0	3-0	4-1		3-0	3-1		1-1	2-2	2-1	0-1		2-1	5-1	2-1	2-0	0-1		3-4	1-0	■

National League South

Season 2019/2020

Team	P	W	D	L	F	A	Pts	PPG
Wealdstone	33	22	4	7	69	35	70	2.12
Havant & Waterlooville	34	19	10	5	64	37	67	1.97
Weymouth	35	17	12	6	60	35	63	1.80
Bath City	35	18	9	8	50	37	63	1.80
Slough Town	35	17	9	9	51	38	60	1.71
Dartford	34	16	8	10	64	46	56	1.65
Dorking Wanderers	35	14	8	13	58	56	50	1.43
Hampton & Richmond	33	14	5	14	51	50	47	1.42
Maidstone United	33	12	9	12	48	44	45	1.36
Chelmsford City	34	11	11	12	55	56	44	1.29
Hemel Hempstead Town	34	12	8	14	36	43	44	1.29
Welling United	34	12	6	16	38	46	42	1.24
Oxford City	34	11	9	14	47	60	42	1.24
Chippenham Town	35	10	12	13	39	45	42	1.20
Tonbridge Angels	31	9	9	13	46	54	36	1.16
Concord Rangers	32	10	7	15	44	48	37	1.16
Billericay Town	32	8	13	11	46	55	37	1.16
Eastbourne Borough	33	8	14	11	38	54	38	1.15
Dulwich Hamlet	35	9	10	16	51	50	37	1.06
St. Albans City	35	9	10	16	41	54	37	1.06
Braintree Town	35	10	5	20	44	67	35	1.00
Hungerford Town	33	8	4	21	38	64	28	0.85

Play was suspended on 16th March 2020 due to the Covid-19 pandemic and then ended early on 20th April 2020. Final league positions were therefore decided on a Points won Per Game basis.

National League South Promotion Play-offs

Slough Town	0	Dartford	3
Bath City	1	Dorking Wanderers	2

Havant & Waterlooville	1	Dartford	2
Weymouth	3	Dorking Wanderers	2

Weymouth	0	Dartford	0

Weymouth won 3-0 on penalties.

Promoted: Wealdstone and Weymouth

There was no relegation out of the National League this season.

2019/2020 Season	Ashton United	Atherton Collieries	Bamber Bridge	Basford United	Buxton	FC United of Manchester	Gainsborough Trinity	Grantham Town	Hyde United	Lancaster City	Matlock Town	Mickleover	Morpeth Town	Nantwich Town	Radcliffe	Scarborough Athletic	South Shields	Stafford Rangers	Stalybridge Celtic	Warrington Town	Whitby Town	Witton Albion
Ashton United	▓	2-2				1-2	3-1			1-0	1-1	3-1		0-4	0-3	2-0	0-2	2-1	0-2	1-1	0-1	3-1
Atherton Collieries		▓	4-1	1-3	1-1	2-3	1-3	2-0	2-1	2-1		1-3	1-5	3-1					3-0	2-4		
Bamber Bridge	3-2	3-0	▓	1-3	2-1	3-0		2-1		1-2	3-2	3-0	2-2	2-1	1-2	1-2	2-0	2-3	3-3			1-1
Basford United	3-2	2-1	3-0	▓	0-2	1-1	4-3	0-0	1-4	4-1	0-1		1-0	0-2	1-0	0-1		3-1	3-0		3-3	1-0
Buxton	1-2		1-1		▓	2-2	3-3	7-0	1-2	1-1		0-1	2-3	1-2		5-0	1-2	5-1	0-0		3-4	2-0
FC United of Manchester		1-0	1-3	7-0		▓	2-2	4-0	1-2	3-2	5-2	3-3	4-2		3-2	0-1	0-2	2-1		4-4		
Gainsborough Trinity		0-2	4-1	1-0	0-0		▓		2-4	2-1	2-2	0-1	0-0	4-1	2-3	1-4		1-3	0-0	2-0	3-1	
Grantham Town	0-4		1-0	1-0	1-3	3-2	1-5	▓		2-2	0-3		1-1	1-2		4-0	2-1	1-3	2-0	2-0		0-4
Hyde United	3-3		4-1	2-3	3-1	1-5	1-1	3-0	▓	5-2	3-1	2-3	1-1	2-0		0-1		4-0	1-2		0-2	0-0
Lancaster City	3-0	1-0	2-3				0-0	0-1	3-3	▓	2-2		1-0	4-1	0-0	1-0	1-2	2-1	0-0	2-1	1-3	1-1
Matlock Town		1-1	1-0	0-1	2-4		2-1	2-2	1-1		▓	3-1	1-1		4-0	1-2	1-2		0-1	1-2	0-2	
Mickleover	0-1			4-2	0-4		4-1		1-3			▓	1-1	2-1	0-1	1-0		1-0	1-0		1-3	1-4
Morpeth Town	1-4	3-0		1-1	2-1				2-1	3-2			▓	1-0	3-1		1-1	1-1		4-0		3-2
Nantwich Town			3-2		2-2	0-1	2-1	2-0	4-0	3-2	3-1			▓	0-1	3-2	0-1	2-1		1-3	3-0	
Radcliffe	1-1	1-0	0-4	3-0			1-1	0-2		3-0	0-3	1-0		2-2	▓	3-1	0-1		1-0	1-1	2-2	1-0
Scarborough Athletic	3-1		5-0	1-1	1-1					1-0	0-1	2-1	4-1	1-0	1-1	▓	3-1	0-0	1-1	1-1	1-1	2-1
South Shields	3-0	3-0	4-1	2-0	1-1	5-3	2-0	1-1	0-1	0-1		5-2		1-4	3-0	2-1	▓			2-1	1-1	1-2
Stafford Rangers			0-0	0-0	0-0	2-2	1-1	1-3	0-3	0-1	0-1	0-2		2-0	1-0	1-2		▓	1-1	2-2	2-1	1-1
Stalybridge Celtic	0-0	1-2	3-2	2-3	2-0	2-3	1-2	3-2			1-3		0-2	1-3	5-1	2-2	0-3		▓	0-2	2-1	
Warrington Town		1-1	3-1	1-1	L	0-1		3-3	4-1	2-2	3-2	1-0	1-3	3-1	1-0	2-0		2-1	1-2	▓	2-1	1-1
Whitby Town	1-1	3-1	0-1			1-2	2-2	1-1	2-0		0-3	1-1	2-1	3-3		2-0	2-1	2-1		0-1	▓	1-1
Witton Albion	1-0	2-1			0-2	3-3	1-0	3-1	2-0	1-3		1-0		1-2		3-1	3-1	2-2	0-1		2-3	▓

Evo-Stik League – Northern Premier Division

Season 2019/2020

	P	W	D	L	F	A	Pts
South Shields	33	21	6	6	64	34	69
FC United of Manchester	32	16	9	7	73	51	57
Warrington Town	32	14	13	5	57	44	55
Basford United	32	16	7	9	49	39	55
Lancaster City	34	15	8	11	58	46	53
Nantwich Town	31	15	7	9	55	39	52
Whitby Town	31	14	8	9	54	42	50
Scarborough Athletic	35	14	8	13	44	47	50
Morpeth Town	27	14	6	7	48	37	48
Hyde United	33	12	7	14	55	55	43
Gainsborough Trinity	32	11	9	12	53	50	42
Stalybridge Celtic	33	12	6	15	42	50	42
Bamber Bridge	33	12	4	17	53	64	40
Witton Albion	31	10	9	12	40	43	39
Mickleover Sports	29	11	5	13	42	52	38
Radcliffe	32	11	5	16	34	50	38
Ashton United	29	10	7	12	40	45	36
Buxton	32	8	11	13	56	52	35
Grantham Town	32	7	9	16	38	71	30
Matlock Town	28	8	5	15	36	43	29
Atherton Collieries	26	8	4	14	36	49	28
Stafford Rangers	33	4	11	18	29	53	23

Ashton United had 1 point deducted for fielding an ineligible player.

Play was suspended during mid-March 2020 due to the effects of the Covid-19 pandemic and the season was subsequently abandoned.

Southern Football League Premier Central 2019/2020 Season

	AFC Rushden & Diamonds	Alvechurch	Banbury United	Barwell	Biggleswade Town	Bromsgrove Sporting	Coalville	Hednesford Town	Hitchin Town	Kings Langley	Leiston	Lowestoft Town	Needham Market	Nuneaton Borough	Peterborough Sports	Redditch United	Royston Town	Rushall Olympic	St Ives Town	Stourbridge	Stratford Town	Tamworth
AFC Rushden & Diamonds			2-1	3-1		2-8	0-3	1-1			5-1	3-0	1-2	2-0		3-0	1-1		1-0	3-2	4-2	
Alvechurch	1-2			2-2	1-1	1-4		0-1	5-0		0-0		1-2	0-2	2-2	0-2	0-1		1-0	0-3		0-2
Banbury United	2-1	2-1		2-1	3-2	0-1	1-1		0-0	1-2		4-2	1-1	0-2	4-2	2-0		1-0	2-0	5-0		0-1
Barwell	0-2	2-1	2-1		3-1	1-3		4-4		3-1	5-0	0-3	1-0	0-1	2-0		3-2	0-0	1-0			1-2
Biggleswade Town	3-1					2-4		1-0	2-0		-	3-0		2-0	0-3	3-1	0-5		2-0	1-2	0-1	2-1
Bromsgrove Sporting	0-0		0-2	1-4	1-1		0-3	4-0	1-2	4-1		6-0	0-1	1-3		7-1	1-1	1-1	3-2	4-1		1-0
Coalville Town	1-0		1-1	4-1	2-0	2-2			2-1	1-2	3-0	1-1		0-1	5-3	1-2		1-4	2-0	1-2		1-1
Hednesford Town	1-1	3-0	2-0				0-1		4-2	1-3		2-1	0-1	0-3	3-3	4-0	4-1			1-2	1-0	0-3
Hitchin Town	1-1	3-1	0-0	4-1		2-2	1-0			0-1		1-3	0-0	1-1	0-2			1-2		1-2	2-0	0-3
Kings Langley	1-0			1-1	2-1	3-1		0-2	3-1		1-2		2-2	2-0	2-2		0-1	4-0		1-4	1-0	
Leiston	2-3	1-2	1-5	1-1	0-4	0-8	1-1	0-3	3-1	0-4			2-1	1-1	2-4			2-2	4-4	0-1		1-2
Lowestoft Town		4-0	0-0	3-2	2-1	0-1	2-1	0-2		2-1	1-3		0-2	0-2		6-0	0-1	0-0	1-0	2-1	2-0	
Needham Market		1-1	0-1	2-3	0-1	0-3		4-3	1-1		3-0	1-0			1-3	2-1	2-2		1-1	1-1	3-3	1-0
Nuneaton Borough	0-1	3-2	2-2	3-1	2-2		0-0			0-3		4-1	1-0			0-3	3-0	2-2	1-3	4-0	4-0	2-0
Peterborough Sports		3-0	1-3	5-4	1-1	3-2			0-4	2-2	8-1	3-1	0-0	2-1		7-0		1-1	5-0	2-2	6-0	4-2
Redditch United	1-1	2-3	0-0	0-1	0-2		2-3	0-1	0-2	0-2	0-6	5-3	0-3	3-2			0-3	0-1			0-2	0-2
Royston Town		3-0	1-0		3-0		1-1	1-0	1-1		0-0	5-1	1-0		4-1	2-1			2-1	5-0	3-1	1-2
Rushall Olympic	1-1	2-0	1-1	0-1	3-2		0-2	1-0	4-2	0-1	6-0	4-1			0-2	3-1	1-3		4-3	2-0	4-1	
St Ives Town	3-4			0-3		1-2	1-1	0-3	2-1	1-0	2-5		2-0	0-3	2-1	0-4	2-4			0-2	2-2	1-1
Stourbridge		1-0	1-1	1-1		2-1	1-1	0-3	1-2	1-3	5-1	2-0			1-6	1-0		2-1	3-1		3-1	
Stratford Town	3-1	2-0		1-5	1-2	1-2	1-4	4-1	3-3	3-3	3-1	0-3	2-1			2-0		1-2		1-2		1-3
Tamworth	3-0	2-0			4-0	1-3		0-1	1-0	2-0	1-2	4-1	1-2	3-3	3-1	3-0	2-0	2-1	3-0		4-1	

Evo-Stik Southern Premier
Premier Division Central

Season 2019/2020

	P	W	D	L	F	A	Pts
Peterborough Sports	33	19	8	6	90	46	65
Tamworth	30	21	2	7	63	27	65
Royston Town	30	19	6	5	62	28	63
Bromsgrove Sporting	32	17	6	9	80	43	57
Rushall Olympic	33	15	8	10	58	43	53
Stourbridge	32	16	5	11	53	52	53
Banbury United	32	14	10	8	48	31	52
Coalville Town	30	14	9	7	51	32	51
Nuneaton Borough	33	14	8	11	57	46	50
Kings Langley	30	15	5	10	51	41	50
AFC Rushden & Diamonds	30	14	7	9	50	45	49
Barwell	32	14	6	12	58	54	48
Needham Market	33	13	9	11	43	40	48
Hednesford Town	32	14	5	13	50	44	47
Biggleswade Town	30	13	4	13	44	45	43
Lowestoft Town	33	13	2	18	48	62	41
Hitchin Town	32	10	9	13	43	49	39
Stratford Town	33	8	4	21	42	74	28
Leiston	32	6	8	18	39	87	26
St. Ives Town	33	6	5	22	33	76	23
Alvechurch	30	4	5	21	25	58	17
Redditch United	33	3	3	27	24	89	12

Play was suspended during mid-March 2020 due to the effects of the Covid-19 pandemic and the season was subsequently abandoned.

78

Southern Football League Premier South 2019/2020 Season	Beaconsfield Town	Blackfield & Langley	Chesham United	Dorchester Town	Farnborough	Gosport Borough	Harrow Borough	Hartley Wintney	Hayes & Yeading United	Hendon	Metropolitan Police	Merthyr Town	Poole Town	Salisbury	Swindon Supermarine	Taunton Town	Tiverton Town	Truro City	Wimborne Town	Walton Casuals	Weston-super-Mare	Yate Town
Beaconsfield Town	■	2-0	1-3	3-1	1-3	0-1		1-2	2-3		1-2	0-0	2-1		0-0		4-0	0-1	0-4	1-2	2-2	1-1
Blackfield & Langley	0-1	■	0-2	2-1	2-0	0-0	2-0	0-0		2-2	3-4	0-0	1-1				0-1	0-2	1-0	2-2	2-1	2-0
Chesham United	3-0	2-1	■	6-3	2-0	3-0	1-1	1-2	3-2	2-1		2-0	2-1	2-0	1-2	1-1		2-1	1-0			4-2
Dorchester Town	1-0	2-2		■		1-2	2-3	2-3	0-3	0-3	0-0	0-1	0-5	1-1	2-2	1-5	2-3	1-0	2-2	1-2	2-0	
Farnborough	2-0	1-1		3-1	■	0-1	1-1		0-1	4-0		1-0	1-4	0-0	0-1	4-0	0-7	0-2	2-1	2-1		4-0
Gosport Borough	0-0		2-1	4-4		■	1-0	0-1	1-1	1-0	2-1	2-2	0-2	0-0		3-0		1-0		2-1	1-0	1-1
Hartley Wintney	1-2	3-1	2-2		0-2			■	1-4	3-2		1-2	1-0	0-0	2-2	2-3	1-1	1-5	1-2	0-1	2-0	0-4
Harrow Borough		1-2	2-0		0-0	1-1	■	1-5			3-0		1-2		1-4			2-2	1-0			
Hayes & Yeading United	1-1	6-0		5-0	2-0	2-1	2-3		■	3-2	0-2		1-2	1-0	1-0	2-2	0-0	0-1	3-1		1-2	2-1
Hendon	2-1		3-1	1-3		2-1	0-1	2-2		■	1-1	2-1	1-3	0-3			1-2	1-4	1-1	2-0	4-0	2-1
Metropolitan Police	3-1	2-0	2-1		1-2	0-0	1-3	0-1		0-3	■	1-2		3-2	2-3	1-1		0-2	2-2	0-3	2-1	2-0
Merthyr Tydfil	0-0	2-0	1-3		2-0	1-0	2-2	3-2	1-2		1-2	■	1-1	3-1	4-2		3-1	0-2	1-1	2-1		
Poole Town	3-1			3-1		3-1					1-1		■	2-0	0-1	1-2		3-1				3-0
Salisbury		1-1	3-2	4-1		1-0	3-1	2-0		2-0	1-3	2-1	2-1	■	0-2	2-1	2-2	0-3	3-1			3-2
Swindon Supermarine		3-0	2-1	1-0	3-2	1-0		3-2	1-1	2-0		2-2	0-1	2-2	■	1-2		1-3		3-2	3-2	
Taunton	3-0	4-1	3-2		3-1	3-2	3-2		2-1	3-3	4-3			1-1		■	3-1	2-0	3-0		1-2	0-4
Tiverton Town	6-1			2-1		2-3			2-0	2-2		2-1	1-0	0-1	3-3	2-0	■	3-2		2-2	2-2	0-2
Truro City		0-1	3-0	2-1	1-0	4-1	2-1	3-0	2-1	4-0		3-3		1-0	1-1	3-3	■		5-1	0-2		
Wimborne Town	2-0	2-0	1-2	2-1		1-2		0-0		0-2		0-0	2-1		0-2	0-3	2-2	■		4-1	2-1	2-0
Walton Casuals		2-3	1-6		0-2	1-1	1-2	0-3	2-3	1-1		2-1	0-3	2-1	2-4	1-5	1-3		0-2	■	2-1	1-1
Weston-super-Mare	1-0		1-2	6-0	1-3		1-1	2-1	1-5	2-2			1-1	3-3		3-2	3-2	5-0	1-0		■	
Yate Town		1-4	4-1		0-1		2-1	2-1	0-2	2-2	1-0		1-1	2-4	2-0	4-1		0-3		0-2	1-2	■

Evo-Stik Southern Premier
Premier Division South

Season 2019/2020

	P	W	D	L	F	A	Pts
Truro City	31	21	4	6	65	30	67
Chesham United	33	21	3	9	70	44	66
Hayes & Yeading United	32	17	6	9	65	42	57
Swindon Supermarine	32	17	6	9	50	41	57
Tiverton Town	29	16	7	6	69	41	55
Taunton Town	31	15	8	8	63	53	53
Salisbury	30	14	9	7	57	42	51
Gosport Borough	33	13	10	10	35	32	49
Poole Town	27	14	6	7	46	28	48
Weston-super-Mare	29	13	6	10	54	45	45
Metropolitan Police	30	13	4	13	46	48	43
Farnborough	30	13	3	14	41	43	42
Merthyr Town	31	9	11	11	37	37	38
Hendon	31	10	8	13	47	51	38
Wimborne Town	33	10	7	16	39	52	37
Hartley Wintney	27	10	6	11	38	39	36
Harrow Borough	34	9	9	16	44	62	36
Blackfield & Langley	31	8	9	14	33	50	33
Yate Town	31	8	5	18	38	56	29
Walton Casuals	33	7	6	20	40	71	27
Beaconsfield Town	32	6	7	19	29	54	25
Dorchester Town	32	4	6	22	36	81	18

Play was suspended during mid-March 2020 due to the effects of the Covid-19 pandemic and the season was subsequently abandoned.

	Bishop's Stortford	Bognor Regis Town	Bowers & Pitsea	Brightlingsea Regent	Carshalton Athletic	Cheshunt	Corinthian-Casuals	Cray Wanderers	East Thurrock United	Enfield Town	Folkestone Invicta	Haringey Borough	Hornchurch	Horsham	Kingstonian	Leatherhead	Lewes	Margate	Merstham	Potters Bar Town	Wingate & Finchley	Worthing
Bishop's Stortford		3-1	2-2			3-2	1-3	1-5	1-0	0-1		1-2	0-2	2-0	1-2	0-1	0-2	2-2		1-4	0-1	0-1
Bognor Regis Town			3-2	0-2	1-2		7-2		4-1	4-3	2-0		1-1	1-1	5-1		1-2	2-1	0-4			0-3
Bowers & Pitsea	2-0	1-2		7-0	0-1		0-2	1-2	1-2	0-1	3-1	3-2	0-1			3-0		0-1	1-1		1-1	1-2
Brightlingsea Regent	1-0		2-4			1-1	2-1	0-2		0-2	0-0		1-0	0-4	0-2		2-3	1-1	0-0	0-0	1-1	0-3
Carshalton Athletic	4-2	1-0		2-0		2-0		4-0	1-2	2-0	1-1		1-4	4-0	2-2	1-0	1-1	1-0	1-1	5-1	3-2	1-2
Cheshunt	0-1		1-1		0-1		1-1		2-3		0-1		0-1	3-1	1-3	0-2	1-2	3-0	2-0		1-0	1-2
Corinthian-Casuals		1-1	0-1	0-1	2-3	3-1		2-1		0-1		1-1	1-2		3-0	1-0	1-2	0-1		0-0	3-3	
Cray Wanderers		3-1	1-0		6-1	0-0			1-1	3-5	2-3	1-1	1-1	2-1	0-0	0-1	2-1	3-2	3-1	4-0	0-0	2-2
East Thurrock United		3-0	3-1	2-1	2-0	4-1		0-1			1-3	4-2			3-3	3-0	1-0	1-2		1-3	3-1	0-0
Enfield Town	5-0	2-0	0-4	2-2	2-1	2-1	3-1	2-3			1-3	5-3	1-1	1-4			1-1		2-0	2-2	2-2	
Folkestone Invicta	1-0	1-2		3-2	1-3	4-2	3-1		4-1	1-1		1-1	2-1	2-1	1-1	1-1		4-0	3-1		0-1	2-0
Haringey Borough	2-1	2-1	1-1	5-1	2-2		1-0		2-0				1-1	1-2	0-1		0-1	1-0		3-2	2-1	2-2
Hornchurch	4-0	0-0	2-1	3-0		3-0	1-1			4-0	1-0	2-1			2-1	3-0	1-1		2-2	2-2	3-1	2-0
Horsham	3-3	0-2	4-0		2-2	2-0	1-0	1-1	1-0		0-1	2-0	1-0			1-1	3-0	0-3	4-0	2-0	2-1	L
Kingstonian	0-3	0-1	0-0	2-1	3-1	2-4	3-1	0-0	0-0	0-0				1-1			3-1	3-3	4-0			0-0
Leatherhead	3-1	1-2	1-0	1-0	2-1	3-0	2-1		3-0	1-2		2-3	2-1		1-1		1-4		0-0	4-0		L
Lewes		0-1	0-2	0-1	0-1	1-6	1-0	2-3	0-3	1-1	0-0	2-1	0-0	0-2	1-2	0-1			3-3		1-2	1-3
Margate	3-4	1-6	1-0	0-0	1-1		2-2	3-4	0-1	0-3		4-2	2-2			0-0	2-0		2-1	2-2	1-0	0-2
Merstham	2-2	2-2	1-3				1-2	2-1	1-4	0-4	1-0	1-2	1-0	0-1	1-4	2-4	1-0			2-3		1-3
Potters Bar Town	1-0	0-1	0-2	4-2	2-0		3-1	1-1		1-2	1-4		2-1	0-2	1-2			2-1				1-1
Wingate & Finchley	1-2	0-5	2-2	0-0	0-2	1-2		0-1	2-1		1-1	1-0	2-3		1-1	1-2	1-1		0-4	1-2		2-3
Worthing		3-0		3-0	1-1	2-0	2-0	1-2	2-3	3-2	0-1		0-6	3-0	2-1	5-5	3-1	2-1	6-1	1-1	4-2	

Isthmian League Premier Division

Season 2019/2020

Worthing	34	21	8	5	72	41	71
Cray Wanderers	33	18	10	5	63	45	64
Carshalton Athletic	35	18	9	8	59	38	63
Hornchurch	33	17	11	5	62	28	62
Folkestone Invicta	32	18	8	6	60	34	62
Horsham	33	17	6	10	51	35	57
Enfield Town	32	16	8	8	61	51	56
Bognor Regis Town	32	16	5	11	58	46	53
Leatherhead	31	15	7	9	48	42	52
Kingstonian	31	11	14	6	42	36	47
East Thurrock United	30	14	4	12	47	40	46
Margate	33	11	10	12	47	54	43
Potters Bar Town	32	11	8	13	47	56	41
Bowers & Pitsea	33	11	7	15	49	42	40
Haringey Borough	30	11	6	13	44	47	39
Lewes	34	8	7	19	35	55	31
Bishop's Stortford	32	8	4	20	37	63	28
Cheshunt	31	8	3	20	39	59	27
Corinthian-Casuals	31	6	8	17	33	44	26
Wingate & Finchley	33	5	10	18	34	58	25
Merstham	33	6	7	20	34	70	25
Brightlingsea Regent	34	5	10	19	24	62	25

Play was suspended during mid-March 2020 due to the effects of the Covid-19 pandemic and the season was subsequently abandoned.

F.A. Trophy 2019/2020

Qualifying 1	Cambridge City	0	Needham Market	3	
Qualifying 1	Buxton	3	Hyde United	2	
Qualifying 1	Lancaster City	1	Witton Albion	0	
Qualifying 1	Morpeth Town	6	Cleethorpes Town	1	
Qualifying 1	Warrington Town	0	Ashton United	1	
Qualifying 1	Redditch United	4	Corby Town	2	
Qualifying 1	AFC Rushden & Diamonds	0	Banbury United	0	
Qualifying 1	Biggleswade Town	2	Bedworth United	1	
Qualifying 1	Lowestoft Town	2	Coalville Town	4	
Qualifying 1	Basford United	3	Mickleover Sports	0	
Qualifying 1	St. Ives Town	0	Soham Town Rangers	0	
Qualifying 1	Grantham Town	5	Rushall Olympic	3	
Qualifying 1	Tamworth	4	Leiston	0	
Qualifying 1	Sutton Coldfield Town	2	Stafford Rangers	1	
Qualifying 1	Folkestone Invicta	2	Lewes	0	
Qualifying 1	AFC Sudbury	2	Harrow Borough	0	
Qualifying 1	Haywards Heath Town	3	Aylesbury United	1	
Qualifying 1	Carshalton Athletic	3	Merstham	1	
Qualifying 1	Uxbridge	1	Bognor Regis Town	3	
Qualifying 1	Westfield	1	Beaconsfield Town	0	
Qualifying 1	Ashford United	1	Barton Rovers	2	
Qualifying 1	Hornchurch	3	Berkhamsted	1	
Qualifying 1	Haringey Borough	3	Horsham	0	
Qualifying 1	Maldon & Tiptree	3	Cray Wanderers	0	
Qualifying 1	Bishop's Stortford	1	Enfield Town	1	
Qualifying 1	Heybridge Swifts	1	Potters Bar Town	2	
Qualifying 1	Brightlingsea Regent	1	Royston Town	2	
Qualifying 1	Metropolitan Police	4	Tilbury	3	
Qualifying 1	Leatherhead	3	Ware	0	
Qualifying 1	Aveley	3	Bowers & Pitsea	0	
Qualifying 1	Sittingbourne	0	Tooting & Mitcham United	1	
Qualifying 1	Chipstead	3	Canvey Island	3	
Qualifying 1	Whitehawk	4	Hendon	1	
Qualifying 1	Barking	0	Margate	0	
Qualifying 1	Wingate & Finchley	1	Hayes & Yeading United	1	
Qualifying 1	Kingstonian	4	Corinthian-Casuals	2	
Qualifying 1	AFC Dunstable	0	Hastings United	4	
Qualifying 1	Phoenix Sports	3	Kings Langley	5	
Qualifying 1	Cheshunt	1	East Thurrock United	2	
Qualifying 1	Basildon United	5	Chesham United	3	
Qualifying 1	Worthing	2	Walton Casuals	1	
Qualifying 1	Melksham Town	1	Basingstoke Town	0	
Qualifying 1	Thame United	1	Frome Town	2	
Qualifying 1	Marlow	0	Sholing	0	
Qualifying 1	Salisbury	3	Dorchester Town	3	
Qualifying 1	Wimborne Town	2	Taunton Town	2	
Qualifying 1	Gosport Borough	3	Farnborough	1	
Qualifying 1	AFC Totton	3	Weston-super-Mare	2	(aet)
Qualifying 1	Kidsgrove Athletic	0	Colne	1	
Qualifying 1	Prescot Cables	0	Pickering Town	0	
Qualifying 1	Whitby Town	4	Worksop Town	1	
Qualifying 1	Nantwich Town	2	Bamber Bridge	1	
Qualifying 1	Atherton Collieries	3	Scarborough Athletic	2	

Qualifying 1	Runcorn Linnets	5	Pontefract Collieries	3	
Qualifying 1	Dunston	0	Gainsborough Trinity	4	
Qualifying 1	Radcliffe	0	FC United of Manchester	2	
Qualifying 1	Stalybridge Celtic	0	South Shields	2	
Qualifying 1	Leek Town	2	Chasetown	0	
Qualifying 1	Halesowen Town	2	Stamford	2	
Qualifying 1	Stourbridge	2	Nuneaton Borough	1	
Qualifying 1	Peterborough Sports	1	Alvechurch	0	
Qualifying 1	Stratford Town	1	Hednesford Town	2	
Qualifying 1	Bromsgrove Sporting	2	Barwell	7	
Qualifying 1	Yate Town	3	Tiverton Town	3	
Qualifying 1	Poole Town	0	Hartley Wintney	1	
Qualifying 1	Paulton Rovers	1	Larkhall Athletic	1	
Qualifying 1	Swindon Supermarine	1	Thatcham Town	4	
Qualifying 1	Cinderford Town	2	Merthyr Town	2	
Qualifying 1	Carlton Town	1	Matlock Town	2	
Qualifying 1	Tadcaster Albion	0	Workington	1	
Qualifying 1	Truro City	1	Blackfield & Langley	1	
Qualifying 1	Hitchin Town	1	Bedfont Sports	1	
Replay	Banbury United	1	AFC Rushden & Diamonds	2	
Replay	Soham Town Rangers	3	St. Ives Town	0	
Replay	Enfield Town	4	Bishop's Stortford	2	(aet)
Replay	Canvey Island	2	Chipstead	1	
Replay	Margate	2	Barking	0	
Replay	Hayes & Yeading United	2	Wingate & Finchley	1	
Replay	Sholing	2	Marlow	0	
Replay	Dorchester Town	0	Salisbury	3	
Replay	Taunton Town	4	Wimborne Town	1	
Replay	Pickering Town	0	Prescot Cables	3	
Replay	Stamford	0	Halesowen Town	3	
Replay	Merthyr Town	4	Cinderford Town	5	(aet)
Replay	Tiverton Town	3	Yate Town	3	
	Yate Town won 4-1 on penalties.				
Replay	Larkhall Athletic	1	Paulton Rovers	3	
Replay	Blackfield & Langley	3	Truro City	1	
Replay	Bedfont Sports	1	Hitchin Town	1	
	Bedfont Sports won 5-4 on penalties.				
Qualifying 2	Halesowen Town	2	Grantham Town	1	
Qualifying 2	Matlock Town	1	Ashton United	0	
Qualifying 2	Atherton Collieries	2	Morpeth Town	1	
Qualifying 2	Sutton Coldfield Town	1	Hednesford Town	5	
Qualifying 2	Peterborough Sports	2	Whitby Town	0	
Qualifying 2	South Shields	4	AFC Rushden & Diamonds	0	
Qualifying 2	Colne	3	Buxton	1	
Qualifying 2	Runcorn Linnets	1	Prescot Cables	1	
Qualifying 2	FC United of Manchester	3	Basford United	1	
Qualifying 2	Leek Town	1	Workington	3	
Qualifying 2	Tamworth	3	Gainsborough Trinity	5	
Qualifying 2	Margate	0	Tooting & Mitcham United	4	
Qualifying 2	Haringey Borough	2	Canvey Island	1	
Qualifying 2	Yate Town	6	AFC Totton	3	
Qualifying 2	Royston Town	7	Haywards Heath Town	0	

Qualifying 2	Bognor Regis Town	3	East Thurrock United	1
Qualifying 2	Westfield	1	Hartley Wintney	1
Qualifying 2	Basildon United	1	Hornchurch	6
Qualifying 2	Taunton Town	3	Aveley	3
Qualifying 2	Worthing	1	AFC Sudbury	4
Qualifying 2	Hastings United	2	Whitehawk	2
Qualifying 2	Salisbury	2	Kings Langley	1
Qualifying 2	Enfield Town	5	Thatcham Town	0
Qualifying 2	Gosport Borough	4	Melksham Town	2
Qualifying 2	Cinderford Town	1	Potters Bar Town	0
Qualifying 2	Needham Market	1	Leatherhead	2
Qualifying 2	Metropolitan Police	2	Biggleswade Town	2
Qualifying 2	Barwell	3	Redditch United	3
Qualifying 2	Nantwich Town	0	Coalville Town	1
Qualifying 2	Stourbridge	2	Lancaster City	2
Qualifying 2	Carshalton Athletic	5	Frome Town	3
Qualifying 2	Sholing	2	Barton Rovers	1
Qualifying 2	Blackfield & Langley	0	Kingstonian	3
Qualifying 2	Maldon & Tiptree	4	Folkestone Invicta	3
Qualifying 2	Hayes & Yeading United	4	Soham Town Rangers	2
Qualifying 2	Bedfont Sports	0	Paulton Rovers	5
Replay	Aveley	2	Taunton Town	1
Replay	Prescot Cables	1	Runcorn Linnets	2
Replay	Hartley Wintney	2	Westfield	1
Replay	Whitehawk	1	Hastings United	2
Replay	Redditch United	3	Barwell	2
Replay	Biggleswade Town	1	Metropolitan Police	0
Replay	Lancaster City	1	Stourbridge	2
Qualifying 3	Curzon Ashton	3	Kidderminster Harriers	0
Qualifying 3	York City	0	Altrincham	1
Qualifying 3	Workington	0	Farsley Celtic	1
Qualifying 3	Hednesford Town	2	Coalville Town	1
Qualifying 3	Runcorn Linnets	0	FC United of Manchester	3
Qualifying 3	Darlington	2	Gainsborough Trinity	1
Qualifying 3	Blyth Spartans	1	Alfreton Town	1
Qualifying 3	Brackley Town	0	Chester	1
Qualifying 3	Guiseley	0	AFC Telford United	4
Qualifying 3	Matlock Town	2	Redditch United	0
Qualifying 3	Colne	2	Southport	3
Qualifying 3	King's Lynn Town	0	Hereford	0
Qualifying 3	Atherton Collieries	1	Boston United	0
Qualifying 3	Peterborough Sports	0	Kettering Town	3
Qualifying 3	Halesowen Town	1	Gateshead	0
Qualifying 3	Leamington	2	Spennymoor Town	1
Qualifying 3	Dulwich Hamlet	2	Chippenham Town	2
Qualifying 3	Bath City	0	Gosport Borough	0
Qualifying 3	Tonbridge Angels	2	Bognor Regis Town	1
Qualifying 3	Weymouth	1	Hastings United	0
Qualifying 3	Chelmsford City	2	Hungerford Town	1
Qualifying 3	Havant & Waterlooville	3	Cinderford Town	1
Qualifying 3	Carshalton Athletic	2	Tooting & Mitcham United	1
Qualifying 3	Enfield Town	4	Maldon & Tiptree	3

Qualifying 3	Braintree Town	1	Yate Town	2	
Qualifying 3	Biggleswade Town	1	Aveley	4	
Qualifying 3	Kingstonian	2	AFC Sudbury	1	
Qualifying 3	Eastbourne Borough	3	Hartley Wintney	1	
Qualifying 3	Leatherhead	0	Dorking Wanderers	3	
Qualifying 3	Concord Rangers	0	Slough Town	0	
Qualifying 3	Maidstone United	2	Dartford	2	
Qualifying 3	Haringey Borough	1	Hemel Hempstead Town	4	
Qualifying 3	Wealdstone	2	Royston Town	3	
Qualifying 3	Oxford City	1	Hornchurch	1	
Qualifying 3	Welling United	3	St. Albans City	1	
Qualifying 3	Salisbury	4	Hayes & Yeading United	3	
Qualifying 3	Gloucester City	0	Bradford (Park Avenue)	2	
Qualifying 3	Stourbridge	1	South Shields	1	
Qualifying 3	Billericay Town	1	Hampton & Richmond Borough	2	
Qualifying 3	Sholing	0	Paulton Rovers	0	
Replay	Hereford	0	Kingís Lynn Town	3	
Replay	Chippenham Town	1	Dulwich Hamlet	2	
Replay	Slough Town	2	Concord Rangers	3	
Replay	Dartford	0	Maidstone United	1	
Replay	Hornchurch	4	Oxford City	4	
	Hornchurch won 4-1 on penalties.				
Replay	Gosport Borough	2	Bath City	3	(aet)
Replay	Alfreton Town	1	Blyth Spartans	3	
Replay	South Shields	4	Stourbridge	0	
Replay	Paulton Rovers	1	Sholing	2	
Round 1	Solihull Moors	2	Darlington	2	
Round 1	South Shields	2	Southport	2	
Round 1	Bradford (Park Avenue)	2	Halesowen Town	2	
Round 1	Harrogate Town	3	Hartlepool United	2	
Round 1	Stockport County	4	Blyth Spartans	2	
Round 1	Chesterfield	0	Notts County	1	
Round 1	Hednesford Town	0	Chester	0	
Round 1	FC Halifax Town	4	Wrexham	0	
Round 1	Farsley Celtic	2	Altrincham	2	
Round 1	Matlock Town	2	Chorley	2	
Round 1	FC United of Manchester	2	Kettering Town	1	
Round 1	AFC Fylde	1	Curzon Ashton	0	
Round 1	Yeovil Town	3	Welling United	1	
Round 1	Hornchurch	1	Dulwich Hamlet	0	
Round 1	King's Lynn Town	2	Dover Athletic	2	
	King's Lynn Town won 4-2 on penalties.				
Round 1	Carshalton Athletic	3	Aveley	3	
Round 1	Eastleigh	6	Yate Town	1	
Round 1	Tonbridge Angels	2	Hampton & Richmond Borough	2	
Round 1	Barnet	2	Weymouth	1	
Round 1	Chelmsford City	2	Havant & Waterlooville	1	
Round 1	Enfield Town	0	Ebbsfleet United	2	
Round 1	Eastbourne Borough	2	Salisbury	2	
Round 1	Maidenhead United	4	Hemel Hempstead Town	2	
Round 1	Sutton United	1	Dagenham & Redbridge	1	
Round 1	Maidstone United	2	Concord Rangers	3	

Round 1	Torquay United	5	Aldershot Town	1	
Round 1	Dorking Wanderers	3	Bromley	0	
Round 1	Royston Town	2	Boreham Wood	0	
Round 1	Kingstonian	3	Woking	1	
Round 1	AFC Telford United	0	Leamington	5	
Round 1	Atherton Collieries	2	Barrow	2	
Round 1	Bath City	2	Sholing	0	
Replay	Aveley	2	Carshalton Athletic	0	
Replay	Southport	3	South Shields	1	
Replay	Halesowen Town	2	Bradford (Park Avenue)	0	
Replay	Chester	2	Hednesford Town	1	
Replay	Altrincham	1	Farsley Celtic	2	(aet)
Replay	Chorley	2	Matlock Town	2	
	Matlock Town won 4-3 on penalties.				
Replay	Hampton & Richmond Borough	2	Tonbridge Angels	0	
Replay	Dagenham & Redbridge	3	Sutton United	2	(aet)
Replay	Barrow	2	Atherton Collieries	0	
Replay	Salisbury	1	Eastbourne Borough	0	
Replay	Darlington	1	Solihull Moors	0	
Round 2	Dorking Wanderers	1	Stockport County	1	
Round 2	Kingstonian	1	Leamington	1	
Round 2	AFC Fylde	4	Southport	1	
Round 2	Royston Town	3	Chester	0	
Round 2	Darlington	0	Harrogate Town	2	
Round 2	Yeovil Town	4	Hampton & Richmond Borough	0	
Round 2	Ebbsfleet United	1	King's Lynn Town	0	
Round 2	Halesowen Town	2	Maidenhead United	2	
Round 2	Notts County	2	Dagenham & Redbridge	1	
Round 2	Chelmsford City	4	Salisbury	0	
Round 2	Torquay United	1	FC Halifax Town	2	
Round 2	Eastleigh	2	Matlock Town	1	
Round 2	Concord Rangers	1	Bath City	1	
Round 2	Farsley Celtic	1	Barnet	1	
Round 2	Hornchurch	1	Aveley	2	
Round 2	Barrow	7	FC United of Manchester	0	
Replay	Stockport County	0	Dorking Wanderers	4	
Replay	Leamington	1	Kingstonian	0	
Replay	Maidenhead United	1	Halesowen Town	3	
Replay	Bath City	1	Concord Rangers	2	
Replay	Barnet	2	Farsley Celtic	0	
Round 3	Ebbsfleet United	0	Royston Town	2	(aet)
Round 3	Concord Rangers	2	Leamington	2	
	Concord Rangers won 4-3 on penalties.				
Round 3	Harrogate Town	2	Eastleigh	0	
Round 3	FC Halifax Town	0	Halesowen Town	1	
Round 3	Barnet	3	Barrow	0	
Round 3	Dorking Wanderers	2	AFC Fylde	4	
Round 3	Aveley	3	Chelmsford City	1	
Round 3	Yeovil Town	1	Notts County	2	

Round 4	Barnet	1	Halesowen Town	2	(aet)
Round 4	Notts County	5	Aveley	0	
Round 4	AFC Fylde	2	Harrogate Town	3	(aet)
Round 4	Concord Rangers	2	Royston Town	1	(aet)
Semi-final	Concord Rangers	2	Halesowen Town	1	

Originally scheduled for March 2020, the two-legged semi-finals were postponed due to the COVID-19 pandemic. The FA declared their intention to complete the tournament and the semi-finals were eventually played during the first half of September as single matches, with a date of 27th September set for the final at Wembley. The final, alongside the FA Vase and held as part of the same event, will be among the matches trialling the return of spectators to elite football after the height of the first-wave of the pandemic in the UK.

F.A. Vase 2019/2020

Round 1	Haughmond	1	Loughborough University	3	(aet)
Round 1	Biggleswade United	4	Saffron Walden Town	4	(aet)
Round 1	Sporting Club Thamesmead	1	Ascot United	5	
Round 1	Jarrow	1	Vauxhall Motors	2	(aet)
Round 1	Bottesford Town	4	West Allotment Celtic	2	(aet)
Round 1	Nostell Miners Welfare	0	Wythenshawe Town	2	
Round 1	Seaham Red Star	1	Yorkshire Amateur	3	
Round 1	Thornaby	4	Billingham Town	0	
Round 1	Shildon	2	West Didsbury & Chorlton	0	
Round 1	Longridge Town	4	Crook Town	2	
Round 1	Knaresborough Town	2	Stockton Town	3	(aet)
Round 1	Penistone Church	1	Bridlington Town	2	
Round 1	Rylands	3	Bootle	0	
Round 1	Selby Town	5	Cheadle Town	1	
Round 1	Padiham	0	Bishop Auckland	1	
Round 1	Abbey Hey	0	Barnoldswick Town	5	
Round 1	Ryhope Colliery Welfare	2	Ashton Athletic	0	
Round 1	Chadderton	1	Guisborough Town	3	
Round 1	Winterton Rangers	2	Consett	5	
Round 1	Maine Road	4	Glasshoughton Welfare	2	(aet)
Round 1	Charnock Richard	2	Lower Breck	5	
Round 1	Grimsby Borough	4	Hemsworth Miners Welfare	0	
Round 1	Leicester Road	1	Walsall Wood	2	(aet)
Round 1	Droitwich Spa	2	Whitchurch Alport	0	
Round 1	Newark Flowserve	2	Heather St. John's	1	
Round 1	GNP Sports	2	Malvern Town	4	(aet)
Round 1	Alsager Town	1	Lutterworth Town	2	
Round 1	South Normanton Athletic	1	Holbeach United	0	
Round 1	Kimberley Miners Welfare	0	Sherwood Colliery	4	
Round 1	Lichfield City	1	Dudley Town	2	(aet)
Round 1	Atherstone Town	3	Sandbach United	1	
Round 1	Brackley Town Saints	2	West Bridgford	3	(aet)
Round 1	Shawbury United	0	Uttoxeter Town	0	
Round 1	Heanor Town	3	Boldmere St Michaels	0	
Round 1	Gresley	0	Rugby Town	1	
Round 1	Pinchbeck United	0	Worcester City	3	
Round 1	AFC Mansfield	2	Hanley Town	1	(aet)
Round 1	Dunkirk	2	Hucknall Town	1	
Round 1	Racing Club Warwick	2	Long Eaton United	3	
Round 1	Clay Cross Town	3	Cottesmore Amateurs	1	
Round 1	Barrow Town	1	Congleton Town	2	
Round 1	Quorn	5	Rocester	3	
Round 1	New Salamis	1	Eynesbury Rovers	6	
Round 1	March Town United	0	Rothwell Corinthians	1	
Round 1	Stansted	5	Aylesbury Vale Dynamos	1	
Round 1	Risborough Rangers	0	FC Clacton	2	
Round 1	Tring Athletic	1	Woodbridge Town	3	
Round 1	Broadfields United	1	Walthamstow	3	
Round 1	Mildenhall Town	4	Crawley Green	1	
Round 1	Norwich United	4	Peterborough Northern Star	1	(aet)
Round 1	AFC Hayes	1	FC Broxbourne Borough	3	
Round 1	Flackwell Heath	2	Colney Heath	3	(aet)
Round 1	Leighton Town	2	Hadleigh United	1	
Round 1	Hadley	0	Milton Keynes Robins	2	

Round 1	Wroxham	6	Baldock Town	2	
Round 1	Northampton ON Chenecks	2	Kirkley & Pakefield	3	(aet)
Round 1	Whitton United	1	Long Buckby	3	
Round 1	Huntingdon Town	2	Frenford	3	(aet)
Round 1	Wellingborough Town	4	Takeley	3	
Round 1	Oxhey Jets	7	Hackney Wick	0	
Round 1	Harborough Town	4	Enfield	1	
Round 1	Coggeshall United	1	Brantham Athletic	0	
Round 1	Lopes Tavares	2	Stanway Rovers	3	
Round 1	Chatham Town	1	Beckenham Town	1	
Round 1	Raynes Park Vale	A	Horndean	A	

The match was abandoned in the 68th minute, with the scoreline 0-0, due to a waterlogged pitch.

Round 1	Sheppey United	0	Corinthian	2	
Round 1	Peacehaven & Telscombe	3	Glebe	5	
Round 1	Welling Town	5	Erith & Belvedere	1	
Round 1	Bedfont & Feltham	3	Colliers Wood United	1	
Round 1	Fisher	3	Greenwich Borough	0	
Round 1	Punjab United	0	Newhaven	3	
Round 1	Mile Oak	1	Redhill	2	
Round 1	Seaford Town	1	Horley Town	0	
Round 1	Rusthall	0	Lancing	2	
Round 1	Sutton Common Rovers	5	Snodland Town	1	
Round 1	Eastbourne Town	4	Horsham YMCA	2	
Round 1	Christchurch	3	Brimscombe & Thrupp	1	
Round 1	Bradford Town	1	Lymington Town	0	
Round 1	Cullompton Rangers	0	AFC Portchester	1	
Round 1	Newport IW	0	Bridgwater Town	2	
Round 1	Westbury United	0	Badshot Lea	1	
Round 1	Malmesbury Victoria	3	Roman Glass St. George	5	
Round 1	Torpoint Athletic	1	Saltash United	4	
Round 1	Tavistock	4	Shepton Mallet	1	
Round 1	Warminster Town	3	East Cowes Victoria Athletic	2	
Round 1	Longlevens	1	Cowes Sports	0	(aet)
Round 1	Bishop's Cleeve	2	Brockenhurst	3	
Round 1	Helston Athletic	1	Falmouth Town	5	
Round 1	Camelford	1	Buckland Athletic	2	
Round 1	Downton	0	Thornbury Town	4	
Round 1	Shrivenham	2	Fairford Town	3	
Round 1	Exmouth Town	2	Portland United	0	
Round 1	Newton Abbot Spurs	0	Westfields	8	
Round 1	White Ensign	4	Buckingham Athletic	1	
Round 1	Southall	4	Tunbridge Wells	4	
Round 1	Kennington	4	Crowborough Athletic	2	
Round 1	Egham Town	0	Binfield	4	
Round 1	Raynes Park Vale	2	Horndean	2	
Round 1	Bitton	6	Tadley Calleva	1	
Round 1	Bournemouth	1	Petersfield Town	2	
Round 1	Romsey Town	1	Plymouth Parkway	3	
Round 1	Westside	3	Deal Town	4	
Round 1	Bovey Tracey	3	Abingdon United	1	

Bovey Tracey were disqualified for fielding an ineligible player.

Replay	Uttoxeter Town	4	Shawbury United	0	
Replay	Saffron Walden Town	5	Biggleswade United	1	
Replay	Tunbridge Wells	1	Southall	3	
Replay	Beckenham Town	2	Chatham Town	2	

Chatham Town won 7-6 on penalties.

Replay	Horndean	1	Raynes Park Vale	2	

88

Round 2	Bishop Auckland	0	West Auckland Town	1	(aet)
Round 2	Hebburn Town	3	Sunderland RCA	0	
Round 2	Irlam	2	Consett	5	
Round 2	Congleton Town	3	Maine Road	2	
Round 2	Stockton Town	2	Barnoldswick Town	0	
Round 2	Northwich Victoria	5	Wythenshawe Town	5	
Round 2	Lower Breck	2	Shildon	1	
Round 2	Vauxhall Motors	4	Ryhope Colliery Welfare	1	
Round 2	Yorkshire Amateur	5	Bottesford Town	4	
Round 2	Newcastle Benfield	4	Guisborough Town	0	
Round 2	Rylands	0	Grimsby Borough	1	
Round 2	Longridge Town	6	Thornaby	4	
Round 2	Newark Flowserve	3	Rugby Town	0	
Round 2	Lye Town	2	Droitwich Spa	1	
Round 2	Wellingborough Town	1	Dudley Town	0	
Round 2	AFC Mansfield	3	Long Buckby	1	
Round 2	West Bridgford	0	Heanor Town	2	
Round 2	Sporting Khalsa	3	Quorn	1	
Round 2	Coventry United	1	Long Eaton United	0	
Round 2	Harborough Town	1	Atherstone Town	6	
Round 2	Woodbridge Town	5	Godmanchester Rovers	2	
Round 2	Norwich United	1	Kirkley & Pakefield	2	
Round 2	Stansted	1	Mildenhall Town	0	
Round 2	Newport Pagnell Town	4	Coggeshall United	2	
Round 2	Saffron Walden Town	3	FC Clacton	4	
Round 2	Leighton Town	6	FC Broxbourne Borough	1	
Round 2	Deeping Rangers	1	Stanway Rovers	3	
Round 2	Milton Keynes Robins	1	Eynesbury Rovers	6	
Round 2	Colney Heath	0	Stowmarket Town	1	
Round 2	Fisher	1	Glebe	2	
Round 2	Frenford	1	Lancing	3	
Round 2	Raynes Park Vale	0	Sutton Common Rovers	4	
	The match was played at the ground of Sutton Common Rovers.				
Round 2	Binfield	3	Redhill	1	
Round 2	Walthamstow	2	AFC Uckfield Town	3	
Round 2	Corinthian	2	Canterbury City	0	
Round 2	Windsor	1	Eastbourne Town	7	
Round 2	Deal Town	4	Oxhey Jets	1	
Round 2	Welling Town	3	Bedfont & Feltham	1	(aet)
Round 2	Kennington	1	Newhaven	6	
Round 2	Warminster Town	3	AFC Portchester	1	
Round 2	Falmouth Town	3	Longlevens	2	(aet)
Round 2	AFC St Austell	0	Buckland Athletic	1	
Round 2	Brockenhurst	0	Plymouth Parkway	3	
Round 2	Abingdon United	1	Hamworthy United	6	
Round 2	White Ensign	A	Wroxham	A	
	The match was abandoned in the 75th minute due to floodlight failure with Wroxham leading 3-0.				
Round 2	Southall	3	Seaford Town	1	
Round 2	Thornbury Town	1	Cribbs	3	(aet)
Round 2	Lutterworth Town	4	Eastwood Community	2	(aet)
Round 2	Walsall Wood	3	Uttoxeter Town	1	
Round 2	Clay Cross Town	3	Sherwood Colliery	1	
Round 2	Shepshed Dynamo	4	Cadbury Athletic	1	
Round 2	Abbey Rangers	2	Ascot United	1	
Round 2	Christchurch	2	Badshot Lea	1	
Round 2	Petersfield Town	1	Roman Glass St. George	2	
Round 2	Bitton	4	Fairford Town	0	

Round 2	Worcester City	3	Dunkirk	1	
Round 2	White Ensign	2	Wroxham	5	
	The match was played at Wroxham.				
Round 2	Baffins Milton Rovers	2	Bradford Town	3	
Round 2	Tavistock	6	Exmouth Town	1	
Round 2	Leicester Nirvana	1	Westfields	2	
Round 2	Bearsted	0	Chatham Town	1	
Round 2	Malvern Town	5	Loughborough University	4	(aet)
Round 2	Saltash United	0	Bridgwater Town	2	(aet)
	The match was played at Bridgwater Town.				
Round 2	Selby Town	2	Bridlington Town	4	
	The match was played at Bridlington Town.				
Round 2	South Normanton Athletic	3	Rothwell Corinthians	1	
	The match was played at Rothwell Corinthians.				
Replay	Wythenshawe Town	2	Northwich Victoria	1	
Replay	Ascot United	7	Abbey Rangers	0	
Round 3	Bridlington Town	1	Stockton Town	4	(aet)
Round 3	Vauxhall Motors	2	Newcastle Benfield	0	
Round 3	Lower Breck	1	Hebburn Town	5	
Round 3	Wythenshawe Town	1	Consett	1	(aet)
Round 3	Congleton Town	2	Longridge Town	2	(aet)
Round 3	West Auckland Town	2	Yorkshire Amateur	1	
Round 3	Westfields	1	Lutterworth Town	3	
Round 3	Heanor Town	2	Sporting Khalsa	4	
Round 3	Lye Town	0	Walsall Wood	2	
Round 3	Malvern Town	3	Atherstone Town	3	(aet)
Round 3	South Normanton Athletic	2	Clay Cross Town	1	(aet)
Round 3	Newport Pagnell Town	0	Kirkley & Pakefield	2	
Round 3	Wroxham	1	Wellingborough Town	0	(aet)
Round 3	Woodbridge Town	1	Stanway Rovers	1	(aet)
Round 3	Stowmarket Town	4	Stansted	0	
Round 3	FC Clacton	1	Eynesbury Rovers	2	
Round 3	Chatham Town	1	Welling Town	0	
Round 3	Deal Town	2	Southall	0	
Round 3	Glebe	1	Newhaven	0	
Round 3	Corinthian	2	Ascot United	1	
Round 3	Lancing	3	Sutton Common Rovers	3	(aet)
Round 3	Leighton Town	2	Eastbourne Town	1	
Round 3	Binfield	4	AFC Uckfield Town	0	
Round 3	Bradford Town	4	Bridgwater Town	3	(aet)
Round 3	Bitton	2	Cribbs	1	
Round 3	Hamworthy United	1	Plymouth Parkway	4	
Round 3	Christchurch	2	Falmouth Town	1	
Round 3	Tavistock	1	Buckland Athletic	2	
Round 3	Coventry United	4	Grimsby Borough	2	
Round 3	Worcester City	2	Shepshed Dynamo	1	(aet)
Round 3	Roman Glass St. George	1	Warminster Town	2	
Round 3	AFC Mansfield	1	Newark Flowserve	3	
Replay	Stanway Rovers	0	Woodbridge Town	4	
Replay	Longridge Town	2	Congleton Town	0	
Replay	Atherstone Town	10	Malvern Town	0	
Replay	Consett	1	Wythenshawe Town	0	
Replay	Sutton Common Rovers	1	Lancing	0	

90

Round 4	Stockton Town	0	Atherstone Town	1	
Round 4	Vauxhall Motors	0	Hebburn Town	1	
Round 4	Longridge Town	5	Newark Flowserve	1	
Round 4	Consett	3	Lutterworth Town	1	
Round 4	West Auckland Town	1	Walsall Wood	0	
Round 4	South Normanton Athletic	1	Wroxham	3	
Round 4	Sporting Khalsa	2	Kirkley & Pakefield	0	(aet)
Round 4	Stowmarket Town	3	Glebe	0	
Round 4	Chatham Town	1	Corinthian	2	(aet)
Round 4	Eynesbury Rovers	3	Leighton Town	4	
Round 4	Deal Town	1	Binfield	1	
Round 4	Bitton	3	Warminster Town	1	
Round 4	Woodbridge Town	0	Plymouth Parkway	1	
Round 4	Buckland Athletic	1	Bradford Town	2	
Round 4	Christchurch	1	Sutton Common Rovers	2	
Round 4	Worcester City	2	Coventry United	1	
Replay	Binfield	3	Deal Town	3	
	Deal Town won 7-6 on penalties.				
Round 5	Corinthian	3	Sporting Khalsa	0	
Round 5	Bradford Town	1	Leighton Town	3	
Round 5	Consett	2	Deal Town	0	
Round 5	Plymouth Parkway	2	West Auckland Town	1	
Round 5	Longridge Town	0	Hebburn Town	1	(aet)
Round 5	Wroxham	2	Stowmarket Town	0	
Round 5	Bitton	2	Sutton Common Rovers	1	
Round 5	Atherstone Town	1	Worcester City	1	
Replay	Worcester City	1	Atherstone Town	1	
	Atherstone Town won 5-4 on penalties.				
Quarter-final	Wroxham	0	Bitton	4	
Quarter-final	Hebburn Town	2	Plymouth Parkway	0	
Quarter-final	Corinthian	4	Leighton Town	3	
Quarter-final	Atherstone Town	1	Consett	3	(aet)
Semi-final	Consett	1	Bitton	0	(aet)
Semi-final	Corinthian	2	Hebburn Town	2	(aet)
	Hebburn Town won 4-3 on penalties.				

Originally scheduled for March 2020, the two-legged semi-finals were postponed due to the COVID-19 pandemic. The FA declared their intention to complete the tournament and the semi-finals were eventually played early in September as single matches, with a date of 27th September set for the final at Wembley. The final, alongside the FA Trophy and held as part of the same event, will be among the matches trialling the return of spectators to elite football after the height of the first-wave of the pandemic in the UK.

National League Fixtures 2020/2021 Season	Aldershot Town	Altrincham	Barnet	Boreham Wood	Bromley	Chesterfield	Dagenham & Redbridge	Dover Athletic	Eastleigh	FC Halifax Town	Hartlepool United	King's Lynn Town	Maidenhead United	Notts County	Solihull Moors	Stockport County	Sutton United	Torquay United	Wealdstone	Weymouth	Woking	Wrexham	Yeovil Town
Aldershot Town		13/03	09/01	20/03	22/05	09/02	05/12	03/05	27/02	08/12	15/05	06/02	17/11	31/10	28/11	02/04	06/10	27/10	24/04	26/01	26/12	20/02	10/04
Altrincham	14/11		24/04	20/02	17/10	17/11	20/03	06/03	08/05	10/04	09/03	05/12	28/11	01/05	13/10	26/12	09/01	29/05	26/01	03/10	08/12	09/02	02/04
Barnet	17/04	23/01		02/01	14/11	20/03	01/05	13/04	03/10	09/02	17/10	17/11	28/12	08/05	02/04	08/12	29/05	30/01	05/12	13/10	20/02	09/03	28/11
Boreham Wood	12/12	21/11	26/12		23/02	26/01	31/10	27/03	30/01	10/10	05/04	03/05	29/05	16/03	27/02	24/04	13/02	13/03	10/04	01/12	27/10	15/05	09/01
Bromley	30/01	27/02	13/03	17/11		09/01	10/04	06/10	31/10	24/04	03/05	09/02	20/02	29/05	20/03	05/12	26/12	10/10	02/04	27/10	26/01	28/11	08/12
Chesterfield	01/12	23/02	12/12	13/04	17/04		22/05	05/04	13/02	06/02	06/10	28/12	14/11	21/11	02/01	17/10	16/03	03/05	15/05	27/03	10/10	23/01	06/03
Dagenham and Red.	05/04	12/12	06/10	06/03	28/12	30/01		02/01	13/04	15/05	13/02	23/01	09/03	01/12	17/04	14/11	23/02	27/03	10/10	16/03	03/05	29/05	17/10
Dover Athletic	13/10	31/10	26/01	28/11	01/05	05/12	26/12		27/10	02/04	06/02	20/02	09/02	03/10	08/12	08/05	10/04	27/02	13/03	09/01	17/11	20/03	22/05
Eastleigh	17/10	10/10	15/05	22/05	06/03	02/04	26/01	09/03		20/03	14/11	28/11	05/12	09/01	06/02	20/02	24/04	06/10	17/11	26/12	10/04	08/12	09/02
FC Halifax Town	16/03	28/12	01/12	08/05	23/01	29/05	03/10	13/02	12/12		02/01	17/04	30/01	27/10	13/03	01/05	27/03	21/11	31/10	05/04	27/02	13/04	13/10
Hartlepool United	03/10	27/10	27/02	05/12	13/10	01/05	02/04	29/05	13/03	26/12		08/12	08/05	10/04	09/02	28/11	30/01	31/10	09/01	24/04	20/03	17/11	20/02
King's Lynn Town	29/05	05/04	23/02	13/10	01/12	10/04	24/04	21/11	27/03	09/01	16/03		01/05	26/12	08/05	26/01	13/03	12/12	27/10	27/02	31/10	30/01	03/10
Maidenhead United	23/02	27/03	10/04	06/02	21/11	13/03	27/10	01/12	05/04	22/05	10/10	06/10		27/02	31/10	09/01	15/05	16/03	26/12	13/02	24/04	03/05	26/01
Notts County	06/03	06/10	10/10	08/12	06/02	20/02	09/02	15/05	17/04	09/03	28/12	02/01	17/10		13/04	17/11	03/05	23/01	28/11	22/05	05/12	02/04	20/03
Solihull Moors	27/03	03/05	13/02	17/10	12/12	26/12	09/01	16/03	29/05	14/11	01/12	12/10	06/03	26/01		09/03	05/04	23/02	30/01	21/11	15/05	06/10	24/04
Stockport County	13/02	02/01	16/03	23/01	05/04	27/02	13/03	10/10	21/11	06/10	27/03	13/04	17/04	23/02	27/10		12/12	15/05	03/05	31/10	22/05	28/12	06/02
Sutton United	01/05	17/04	06/02	02/04	02/01	08/12	17/11	28/12	23/01	28/11	22/05	14/11	03/10	13/10	05/12	20/03		13/04	20/02	08/05	09/02	06/03	09/03
Torquay United	09/03	06/02	22/05	14/11	08/05	13/10	28/11	17/10	01/05	20/02	06/03	20/03	08/12	24/04	17/11	03/10	26/01		09/02	10/04	02/04	05/12	26/12
Wealdstone	23/01	13/04	05/04	28/12	13/02	03/10	08/05	14/11	23/02	06/03	17/04	09/03	02/01	27/03	22/05	13/10	21/11	01/12		12/12	06/02	17/10	01/05
Weymouth	13/04	15/05	03/05	09/02	09/03	28/11	08/12	17/04	02/01	05/12	23/01	17/10	02/04	30/01	20/02	06/03	10/10	28/12	20/03		06/10	14/11	17/11
Woking	02/01	16/03	21/11	09/03	13/04	08/05	13/10	23/02	28/12	17/10	12/12	06/03	23/01	05/04	03/10	30/01	01/12	13/02	29/05	01/05		17/04	14/11
Wrexham	21/11	01/12	27/10	03/10	27/03	24/04	06/02	12/12	16/03	26/01	23/02	22/05	13/10	13/02	01/05	10/04	31/10	05/04	27/02	13/03	09/01		08/05
Yeovil Town	28/12	13/02	27/03	17/04	16/03	31/10	27/02	30/01	01/12	03/05	21/11	15/05	13/04	12/12	23/01	29/05	27/10	02/01	06/10	23/02	13/03	10/10	

Please note that the above fixtures may be subject to change.

National League North Fixtures 2020/2021 Season	AFC Fylde	AFC Telford United	Alfreton Town	Blyth Spartans	Boston United	Brackley Town	Bradford Park Avenue	Chester	Chorley	Curzon Ashton	Darlington	Farsley Celtic	Gateshead	Gloucester City	Guiseley	Hereford	Kettering Town	Kidderminster Harriers	Leamington	Southport	Spennymoor Town	York City
AFC Fylde		03/05	27/02	16/01	14/11	28/11	01/12	24/04	02/01	23/03	06/10	31/10	13/02	15/05	06/02	10/04	17/10	22/05	20/03	28/12	10/11	02/04
AFC Telford United	09/01		31/10	13/02	27/02	06/10	02/04	26/12	17/11	08/05	27/03	24/04	17/10	13/03	28/11	01/12	10/04	01/05	22/05	07/11	06/02	23/01
Alfreton Town	24/10	17/04		03/05	02/01	10/11	20/03	13/04	12/12	20/02	21/11	14/11	22/05	09/02	15/05	16/01	28/12	06/03	23/03	05/04	10/10	06/02
Blyth Spartans	08/05	10/10	09/01		28/11	10/04	09/02	23/01	22/05	20/03	01/05	10/11	26/12	06/03	20/02	14/11	02/04	17/04	06/02	24/10	23/03	01/12
Boston United	27/03	24/10	26/12	05/04		23/01	06/03	12/12	07/11	29/05	13/03	01/05	08/05	13/04	10/10	30/01	17/11	09/02	20/02	17/04	21/11	09/01
Brackley Town	05/04	20/02	13/03	12/12	15/05		16/01	21/11	06/02	10/10	07/11	22/05	27/03	28/12	17/04	03/05	02/01	17/11	13/04	09/02	24/10	06/03
Bradford Park Avenue	12/04	21/11	07/11	24/04	17/10	08/05		09/01	31/10	01/05	27/02	06/02	05/10	27/03	22/05	13/02	13/03	23/01	12/12	16/11	05/04	26/12
Chester	09/02	02/01	01/12	15/05	10/04	02/04	03/05		28/12	24/10	30/01	23/03	28/11	17/04	14/11	10/11	29/05	20/02	10/10	16/01	06/03	20/03
Chorley	26/12	23/03	10/04	30/01	20/03	29/05	17/04	01/05		01/12	08/05	09/01	23/01	10/10	10/11	02/04	28/11	24/10	14/11	06/03	09/02	20/02
Curzon Ashton	16/11	16/01	05/10	07/11	06/02	13/02	28/12	27/02	12/04		31/10	17/10	13/03	12/12	03/05	24/04	27/03	05/04	21/11	02/01	15/05	22/05
Darlington	20/02	14/11	02/04	28/12	10/11	20/03	24/10	22/05	16/01	17/04		10/04	01/12	06/02	23/03	28/11	15/05	10/10	06/03	03/05	02/01	09/02
Farsley Celtic	17/04	09/02	27/03	13/03	28/12	30/01	29/05	17/11	03/05	06/03	12/12		07/11	05/04	02/01	15/05	16/01	21/11	24/10	13/04	20/02	10/10
Gateshead	10/10	06/03	30/01	02/01	16/01	14/11	20/02	05/04	15/05	10/11	13/04	20/03		24/10	09/02	29/05	03/05	12/12	17/04	21/11	28/12	23/03
Gloucester City	23/01	10/11	24/04	17/10	01/12	01/05	14/11	31/10	13/02	10/04	29/05	28/11	27/02		02/04	23/03	06/10	09/01	26/12	30/01	20/03	08/05
Guiseley	29/05	05/04	23/01	06/10	13/02	31/10	30/01	27/03	13/03	09/01	17/11	26/12	24/04	21/11		17/10	27/02	07/11	08/05	12/12	13/04	01/05
Hereford	12/12	13/04	08/05	27/03	22/05	09/01	10/10	13/03	21/11	09/02	05/04	23/01	06/02	17/11	06/03		07/11	26/12	01/05	20/02	17/04	24/10
Kettering Town	06/03	12/12	01/05	21/11	23/03	26/12	10/11	06/02	05/04	14/11	23/01	08/05	09/01	20/02	24/10	20/03		13/04	09/02	10/10	22/05	17/04
Kidderminster Harr.	30/01	28/12	17/10	31/10	24/04	23/03	15/05	06/10	27/02	28/11	13/02	02/04	10/04	03/05	20/03	02/01	01/12		10/11	29/05	16/01	14/11
Leamington	07/11	30/01	17/11	29/05	06/10	01/12	10/04	13/02	27/03	02/04	17/10	27/02	31/10	02/01	16/01	28/12	24/04	13/03		15/05	03/05	28/11
Southport	01/05	20/03	28/11	27/02	31/10	24/04	23/03	08/05	17/10	26/12	09/01	01/12	02/04	22/05	10/04	06/10	13/02	06/02	23/01		14/11	10/11
Spennymoor Town	13/03	29/05	13/02	17/11	02/04	27/02	28/11	17/10	24/04	23/01	26/12	06/10	01/05	07/11	01/12	31/10	30/01	08/05	09/01	27/03		10/04
York City	21/11	15/05	29/05	13/04	03/05	17/10	02/01	07/11	06/10	30/01	24/04	13/02	17/11	16/01	28/12	27/02	31/10	27/03	05/04	13/03	12/12	

Please note that the above fixtures may be subject to change.

National League South Fixtures 2020/2021 Season	Bath City	Billericay Town	Braintree Town	Chelmsford City	Chippenham Town	Concord Rangers	Dartfird	Dorking Wanderers	Dulwich Hamlet	Eastbourne Borough	Ebbsfleet United	Hampton & Richmond Borough	Havant and Waterlooville	Hemel Hempstead Town	Hungerford Town	Maidstone United	Oxford City	Slough Town	St. Albans City	Tonbridge Angels	Welling United
Bath City	■	10/10	29/05	13/02	02/01	24/04	27/03	10/04	24/10	06/03	06/02	27/02	17/11	07/11	28/12	03/05	16/03	05/04	16/01	15/05	28/11
Billericay Town	20/03	■	28/12	01/12	06/03	02/01	13/02	29/05	16/01	15/05	31/10	28/11	17/10	02/04	03/05	27/02	10/11	14/11	06/02	06/10	13/04
Braintree Town	23/01	13/03	■	26/12	20/03	17/11	09/01	17/10	06/02	24/04	06/10	22/05	03/05	31/10	07/11	13/02	28/11	08/05	10/04	02/04	01/12
Chelmsford City	12/12	08/02	02/01	■	21/11	28/12	15/03	16/01	05/04	27/03	29/05	14/11	20/02	30/01	06/03	24/10	10/10	01/05	15/05	09/11	17/04
Chippenham Town	26/12	22/05	10/10	27/02	■	28/11	24/10	01/05	27/03	30/01	14/11	01/12	09/01	23/01	16/03	08/05	13/04	10/11	05/04	17/04	13/02
Concord Rangers	14/11	26/12	13/04	13/03	20/02	■	22/05	21/11	16/03	12/12	17/04	09/01	23/01	08/05	27/03	05/04	01/05	30/01	10/10	09/02	10/11
Dartford	17/10	12/12	15/05	06/10	02/04	06/03	■	07/11	29/05	09/02	02/01	20/03	31/10	10/04	20/02	24/04	16/01	21/11	17/11	28/12	06/02
Dorking Wanderers	10/11	23/01	27/03	08/05	06/02	27/02	17/04	■	13/04	16/03	28/11	26/12	13/03	09/01	05/04	01/12	24/10	10/10	03/05	14/11	22/05
Dulwich Hamlet	02/04	08/05	01/05	31/10	17/10	06/10	23/01	17/11	■	07/11	20/03	13/03	10/04	27/02	24/04	28/11	13/02	09/01	01/12	30/01	26/12
Eastbourne Borough	22/05	09/01	14/11	17/10	03/05	13/02	01/12	06/10	17/04	■	10/11	02/04	08/05	20/03	06/02	28/12	27/02	23/01	28/11	13/04	31/10
Ebbsfleet United	01/05	05/04	16/03	23/01	24/04	07/11	26/12	20/02	10/10	10/04	■	08/05	12/12	22/05	24/10	17/11	30/01	09/02	27/03	21/11	13/03
Hampton and Rich.	21/11	20/02	06/03	24/04	09/02	15/05	10/10	02/01	28/12	24/10	16/01	■	07/11	17/11	10/04	06/02	05/04	12/12	16/03	29/05	03/05
Havant & Waterloo.	14/04	27/03	30/01	28/11	15/05	29/05	05/04	28/12	11/11	02/01	13/02	17/04	■	02/12	16/01	10/10	14/11	24/10	06/03	01/05	27/02
Hemel Hempstead T.	17/04	24/10	05/04	03/05	29/05	16/01	10/11	15/05	21/11	10/10	06/03	13/04	09/02	■	12/12	27/03	28/12	16/03	02/01	20/02	14/11
Hungerford Town	13/03	30/01	17/04	22/05	06/10	17/10	28/11	31/10	14/11	01/05	02/04	10/11	26/12	13/02	■	09/01	01/12	13/04	27/02	20/03	23/01
Maidstone United	30/01	21/11	12/12	02/04	16/01	31/10	14/11	09/02	20/02	13/03	13/04	01/05	20/03	17/10	15/05	■	06/03	17/04	29/05	02/01	06/10
Oxford City	06/10	10/04	20/02	20/03	17/11	06/02	08/05	02/04	12/12	21/11	03/05	31/10	24/04	13/03	09/02	22/05	■	26/12	07/11	17/10	09/01
Slough Town	31/10	24/04	16/01	06/02	10/04	03/05	27/02	20/03	15/05	29/05	01/12	13/02	02/04	06/10	17/11	07/11	02/01	■	28/12	06/03	17/10
St. Albans City	08/05	01/05	10/11	09/01	31/10	20/03	13/04	30/01	09/02	20/02	17/10	06/10	22/05	26/12	21/11	23/01	17/04	13/03	■	12/12	02/04
Tonbridge Angels	09/01	16/03	24/10	10/04	07/11	01/12	13/03	24/04	03/05	17/11	27/02	23/01	06/02	28/11	10/10	26/12	27/03	22/05	13/02	■	08/05
Welling United	20/02	17/11	09/02	07/11	12/12	10/04	01/05	06/03	02/01	05/04	28/12	30/01	21/11	24/04	29/05	16/03	15/05	27/03	24/10	16/01	■

Please note that the above fixtures may be subject to change.

Supporters' Guides and Tables books

Our Supporters' Guide series has been published since 1982 and the new 2021 editions contain the 2019/2020 Season's results and tables, Directions, Photographs, Telephone numbers, Parking information, Admission details, Disabled information and much more.

Our Football Tables books are perfect companions to the Supporters' Guides and contain historical Football League, Non-League and Scottish final tables up to the end of the 2019/2020 season.

THE SUPPORTERS' GUIDE TO PREMIER & FOOTBALL LEAGUE CLUBS 2021

This 37th edition covers all 92 Premiership and Football League clubs. *Price £9.99*

NON-LEAGUE SUPPORTERS' GUIDE AND YEARBOOK 2021

This 29th edition covers all 67 clubs in Step 1 & Step 2 of Non-League football – the Vanarama National League, National League North and National League South. *Price £9.99*

SCOTTISH FOOTBALL SUPPORTERS' GUIDE AND YEARBOOK 2021

The 28th edition features all Scottish Professional Football League, Highland League and Lowland League clubs. *Price £9.99*

ENGLISH FOOTBALL LEAGUE & F.A. PREMIER LEAGUE TABLES 1888-2020

The 23rd edition contains every Football League & F.A. Premier League final table plus play-off results and F.A. Cup and League Cup semi-final & final results. *Price £9.99*

NON-LEAGUE FOOTBALL TABLES 1889-2020

The 19th edition contains final league tables and historical notes for the 3 Leagues operating at Steps 3 and 4 of the pyramid, the Northern Premier League, Southern League and Isthmian League. This edition also covers the Staffordshire County Senior League 2005-2020. *Price £9.99*

SCOTTISH FOOTBALL TABLES 1890-2020

The 10th edition contains final league tables for all Scottish Professional Football League, Scottish League, Scottish Premier League, Highland League and Lowland Football League seasons plus the East of Scotland Football League. *Price £9.99*

These books are available UK & Surface post free from –

Soccer Books Limited (Dept. SBL)
72 St. Peter's Avenue
Cleethorpes, DN35 8HU
United Kingdom